Joan was born in 1932 in Port Elizabeth, South Africa. Her family settled in George, Western Cape. She was the eldest of three daughters. Tragically, she lost her youngest sister and her father before she turned 18. Always an adventurous, sporting, fun-loving individual, she embarked on this trip and so began a life-long adventure with her soulmate and co-traveller, Carel. They married in London seven months after beginning the trip and eventually raised a family in South Africa. Joan never wrote a book but was a life-long prolific letter writer. After her passing in 2018, her daughter, Louise, put together the stories of this trip, the photographs and the diary to share this inspirational journey. Louise currently lives in Perth, Australia, with her daughter and son.

For Dad and Mum and the trip you started in 1958.
Your pioneer spirit and love for each other is humbling.

Irene Joan Marais and
Louise Marais

1958

Home Is a Journey

AUSTIN MACAULEY PUBLISHERS™
LONDON • CAMBRIDGE • NEW YORK • SHARJAH

All of the events in this memoir are true to the best of author's memory. The views expressed in this memoir are solely those of the author.

A CIP catalogue record for this title is available from the British Library.

ISBN 9781528997645 (Paperback)
ISBN 9781528997652 (Hardback)
ISBN 9781528997669 (ePub e-book)

www.austinmacauley.com

First Published (2021)
Austin Macauley Publishers Ltd
25 Canada Square
Canary Wharf
London
E14 5LQ

Thanks to my parents for being the hoarders that they are so I had a treasure trove of intact photos, letters, souvenirs and the all-important diary that survived 60 years, never getting lost or thrown away during any one of the numerous moves. It has been both a curse and a joy wading through all the information trying to put this book together, what a wonderful legacy to be given! I must thank the van Eeden family for all the support, enthusiasm and help in filling in some of the gaps as documented by their mum, Audrey. To my children, Megan and Ryan, you are the air that I breathe, thank you for giving me time to work on the book when I should have been mum. To my friends, who encouraged, supported and got earache from endless talk of this book, love you madly!

Introduction

From a young age, my parents' trip through Africa filtered into our family's everyday lives. Travel, adventure, doing extraordinary things was often our norm. My first trip overseas in 1976 was when I was 6 years old. I had flown my dad's work airplane and helicopter before age 10 and we could all ski (water and snow) by the age of 10. My dad's work saw us move around South Africa and I had changed towns three times by the time I finished high school.
As kids, we would often watch the cine taken during this trip. Our parents would narrate, with my mum always ensuring factual correctness, my dad only too happy to concede sparing him the need to retain "irrelevant" detail. Their trip lived within them, was an expression of their spirit and was engrained into our lives through the encouragement to do, to take risks, to make changes, to not be afraid of the unknown and to be eternally bored with the ordinary.

This trip came about with my dad, Carel, feeling listless with life. Two years prior, he had completed a similar road trip, Cape to London, with a male companion, Adriaan van Jaarsveld, in a small Renault.

Adriaan, Joan and Carel, Carel's first trans-Africa road trip

After this trip, followed by a brief work posting in the Netherlands, my dad found himself in 1957 working in Klerksdorp, a small town 170 km south of Johannesburg. He started talking to two of his brothers about doing a second trip through Africa, Europe and finishing in London where the three could explore work opportunities. All three brothers at that stage were young, single, qualified engineers.

My dad first met my mum in her home town of George where he was working in the town engineer department, this was a few years prior to 1957. The first time my mum saw him he was working under his old Jaguar and all she saw were his legs sticking out, which she found quite attractive. At the time though he was dating my mum's sister, but this did not work out. He did take my mum dancing and to parties, although they did not date, before setting off on his first trans Africa trip. They kept in contact and in 1957, when my mum went to Klerksdorp to play a provincial hockey match they met up and from there plans were set in motion. My mum had been talking with her friend Audrey about flying to London, these plans got changed with my dad convincing the two ladies to join him and his brothers on the road trip. I am told this had the simple motivation of getting the extra passengers to help pay the petrol costs, but I do believe something had been ignited a few years back in George.

Activities began and it was agreed they needed to leave in January 1958 before the Africa rains started. With a couple of letters and a telegram in late 1957, a car was bought and despite family and friends advising against it, calling it a fool hardy trip, plans went ahead regardless. So began this trip that forged lifelong friendships, a fairy tale marriage and leaving a profound mark on each traveller.

As was fairly normal in those days, my Mum and Audrey kept diaries and recorded each day's travel. Some days the diary entries are ordinary, some describe a world long gone, some describe in an academic way, hardships experienced.

Many years later my brothers and I tried encouraging my parents, specifically my mum, to formally document their journey, however living the everyday life took preference to documenting the past, so a book never materialized. With my mum's passing in 2018, my dad found her diary and passed this onto me asking if I would like to read it or, if not, he was going to destroy it on account of it being her personal writings. Naturally, I read it. This was in January 2019 and I spent the next couple of months typing the diary up, did a trip back to South Africa to collect a treasure trove of letters, photos, slides, postcards, newspaper articles and various memorabilia. Lucky for me, and you the reader, my parents are of an era where you did not throw things away. Putting this book together has been my absolute privilege and was a labour of love. I hope I have captured and done justice to the individuals herein and managed to convey the enormity of the challenges of the trip. My apologies in advance to anyone offended for some political incorrectness. I chose to keep the writing as authentic as I could. This is after all a diary written over 60 years ago by a 26-year-old person not a politician or public relations specialist. There is a human side to the writer, influenced at times with travel fatigue/crankiness and a personal view point.

As you read each day's entry, keep placing yourself in their shoes and imagine how you would fare. Would you have been bold and seized the opportunity, would you have seen each obstacle as an adventure or something to be avoided or a reason to quit. Whatever your tolerance for challenge is, I hope you can find the remarkable in these ordinary everyday writings and see what extraordinary individuals these were who saw adventure where others saw danger or hardship. Life is simply a journey of comfort and discomfort, best tackled with a sense of adventure.

I hope you enjoy this book and it ignites your own imagination or recollection of adventure(s) undertaken.

Let us begin.

The Time and Route Travelled

The group left the Cape, South Africa on the 29th December 1957 and got to Trafalgar Square, London England on the 28th April 1958. It took them 120 days (4 months). The distance covered was about 13,500 miles (21 720 km).

The Travel Companions

Mr Carel Petrus Marais

Civil Engineer, aged 28 at the start of the trip

Born: 14 February 1929, currently 91 years old

Mr Carel Petrus Marais

Mr Johannes Petrus Albertus Marais

Chemical Engineer, aged 31 at the start of the trip

Born: 19 July 1926 and passed away on 25th March 1985 (aged 58)

Mr Johannes Petrus Albertus Marais

Mr Marius Nolte Marais

Civil Engineer aged 25 at the time of the trip

Born: 16 October 1933 passed away on 31st May 2013 (aged 79)

Mr. Marius Nolte Marais

Miss Irene Joan Povall (married Marais)

Bookkeeper aged 25 at the start of the trip

Born: 3rd January 1932 and passed away the 12th February 2018 (aged 86)

Miss Irene Joan Povall

Miss Audrey Hilda Nives (married van Eeden)

Draftswoman and Artist aged 27 at the start of the trip

Born: 4th June 1930 and passed away the 25th September 2019 (aged 89)

Miss Audrey Hilda Nives

The Vehicle

A 1954 Volkswagen type 1 (T1) Kombi (VW Microbus). The T1 split windscreen "splittie", was bought by Carel in South Africa for £600 second hand (3 years old with 1300 miles on it) in late 1957. After the trip, it was shipped back to South Africa and sold in Cape Town in September 1959 for £450. Additions made to it included a roof rack carrier, radio inserted and a canvas tent that was attached off the roof rack. The car had a manual gearbox, the motor was a 1.2 litre, 30 horsepower (hp) air-cooled flat–four cylinder "boxer" engine mounted in the rear.

This car, by modern standards, had no 4 x 4 capability (no diff lock, low or high range gears), no power steering, no air con, no extra height clearance for the undercarriage, no long-range petrol tanks and simply had the horsepower of about three lawn mowers.

Some additional equipment included:

1. Four spare tyres. Tyres were tubed and were prone to regular punctures with the odd burst. They were fixed by taking the tube out and gluing a rubber patch over the leak or with a burst simply replaced.
2. 5.3-gallon tin for water (around 20 litres)
3. 5.3-gallon tin for petrol (around 20 litres)
4. Paraffin
5. Block and tackle
6. Rope
7. Some spares for the car including clutch cable and tyre tubes with the patches and glue
8. Mosquito nets
9. Citronella oil
10. Waterproof groundsheet for the three men to sleep on every night as they slept outside the kombi in the tent. The ladies slept in the kombi which had been modified with a fold away mattress bed
11. Some basic medical supplies (Daraprim was taken every Wednesday for malaria)
12. A compass
13. A trans-African highways, 3rd edition, 1956 printed book

The Menu

Regular food items enjoyed for breakfast, lunch and dinner included:

Fresh bread, butter/margarine, jam, biscuits/Ryvita, various tinned food (bully beef, pilchards, tuna, beans), rice, powdered milk, powdered eggs, fresh vegetables and fruit, the occasional fresh meat, chicken or fish, fresh eggs, cool drink, sugar, tea and coffee.

Pre-Planning an Inventory

For those of you interested, the following telegram and five letters are between Carel and Joan and detail the pre-planning they did before embarking on the trip.

Apparently, you don't need much pre-planning, even for serious trips!

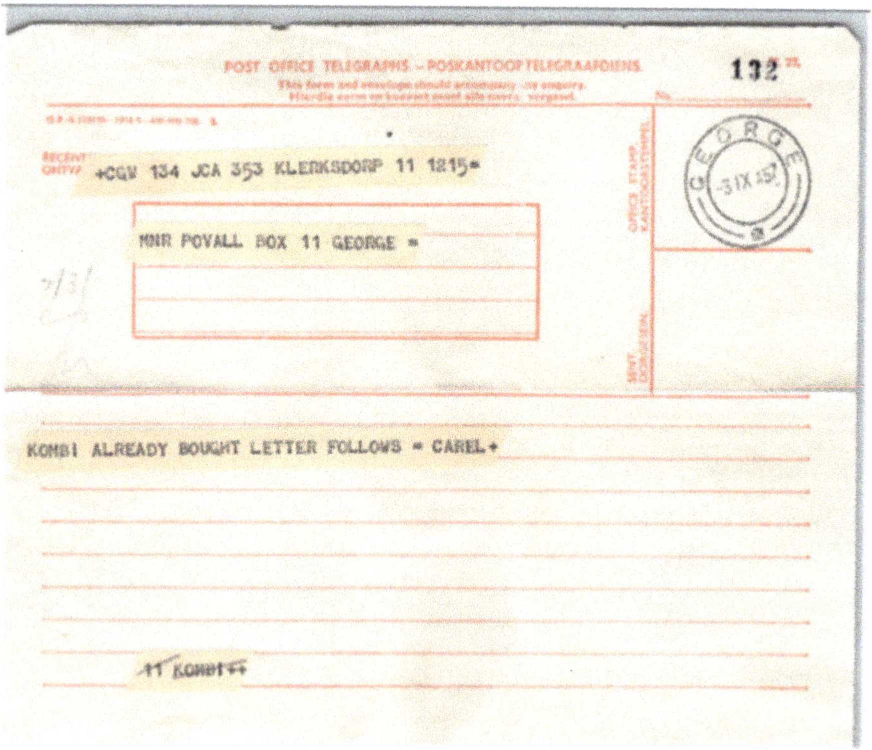

POST OFFICE TELEGRAPHS - POSKANTOORTELEGRAAFDIENS

132

+CGV 134 JCA 353 KLERKSDORP 11 1215=

MNR POVALL BOX 11 GEORGE =

KOMBI ALREADY BOUGHT LETTER FOLLOWS = CAREL+

11 KOMBI++

Box 99,
Klerksdorp.
5 Sept., 1957.

Hullo Joan,

Sorry for the long delay in letting you know about the tour. There were some great decisions to be made this side of the equator.

As I telegraphed I have already bought a kombi, called the skilpad;i.e. our traveling home. It is a second hand car but ha onely done 1500 miles. It is already fitted for touring, with a roof carier, radio and lean to tent. You girls will have the most marvelous bed just like a innersprung matres, while Marius and I will sleep in the tent.

BUSINESS. 1) You are a optimust I'll boss you like mad, SO WHAT '.

2) Clothes. YOU can take much more then you thought, space is no object with the Kombi. If you can stick to 22lb. max. for yourself plus clothes we are O. K. so you can add to your list, remember Africa is darn ed hot and Europe darned cold make provision for both. The aksent is on nilon and kakies for Africa for washing facilities are far and few.You will need a raincoat and awarm coat,and strong but comfortabl shoes.

3) Route: Iam including a map of the route. Let me know which you prefer, Discuss with Adriaan which he advices. I prefer the following route, along the east coast. Lourenso Marques, Beira, Palma, Dares Salaam , Mombasa, Nairobi, Addis Ababa, Asmara, Karthum,and then along the Nile to Cairo. WE may have trouble to get through Ethiopia and the Sudan. In this case we will have to travel right across to the west to get the route through Algeria. I am writing for permision to travel through these two countries.

4) You will have to get the visas for us but Marius and I still have to get our pasports. Marius can get some of the visas becaus he is in Pretoria.

5) Can you get Marius and me Youth Hostel memberships becaus nere in klerksdorp aint a Youth Hostel branch.

6) Dont worry about mosquito-netting, I am still working on a projeck to make the tent and the kombi mosquito proof.

7) As I said before you will take charge of the food department. It may be best if each gets his own knife and fork and plate, and you arrange the rest such as primus (we have room for two) pots and pans (I have one pan and one small pot). Please let me have your list for the food department. A most usefull item is lots of Boerbeskuit Adriaan and I had a parafin tin full and we wished we had more.

8)About the advertising, how about getting some firm to help pay our tour especially the SHELL COMPANY. Last time we wrote them but it was no can do. Now I think we must write to the European office. Can you get their address?,and will you write to them or do you prefer me to write?. I am writing to the Volkswagen factory in Germany to see if they will do our repairs for us if we advertise the Volkswagen. How about asking the Outspan, or LIFE, or The Post if they are interested in an article and foto's of a tour th rough dark Africa, or if you have anny other ideas try them.We'll need the extra money.

9) Aubry can practise her art as much as she likes on the Kombi, onely I want on the front the UNION FLAG and SOUTH AFRICA painted.

10) Wepons: I am taking my pistol with, if you have one take it but it ant really nessesary.

11) Willy you get our medical supplies, you know more about that then I do. For malari a get Palladrene not Quinene, again ask Adriaan.

12) Keep a check of all money spent on non personal items, we'll square up later.

13) I have asked Marius to try and get sleeping bags from the ex army shops in Pretoria . You in the Kombi can take blankets or a sleeping bag, maybe the sleeping bag will be better.

14) It may be better to wait with the curtains. We can come down in December and spend aday or two in George,. Better wait with the food to til then.

15) Have you (by you I mean you and Aubry) a pair of binoculars, or a compas,? it will be most usefull if you have.

16) You can get all the neccessary injections in Mosselbay, make shure you have them all.

17) Are you members of the A. A.?, because it will be good if you can get International Driving Permits., but wait till nearly December before you get it, then it stays longer valid.

2a) Remember to take smart clothes with i. e. clothes for going out, because I intend starting nightclub crawling in Africa already. Dont forget your bathing costumes

REMEMBER in your planing, space is no object in the Kombi but try and keep the weight down as much as possible.

Joan, for the moment that is all that I can think off, later most probably I'll remembe r a lot of other things. I have worked it out again that unless something unforseen happens the tour will cost each of us£80 for peterol and food, entertainment not included.

Now no remarks about my typing, I am practising for the other letters, hard work for the one finger.

my best wishes Joan and Aubry

Carl

P.O. Box 11,
GEORGE.
15th September, 1957.

Dear Carel,

Many thanks for your letter and all the details. How Audrey and I poured over it. We got together last night and drew up the following list. Please don't be too alarmed - but it is a bit difficult trying to imagine everything that has to be done. Anyway we won't let you down as long as you don't mind answering our queries. Firstly I know you have many more letters to answer so don't kill your self answereing this one. The only immediate answere we want is - we can manage to get a lift to Cape Town on the 14th October (coming back on the 20th October, & we both have leave due us) so do you think we should go down to get our Visas etc or should we wait until you and Marius come down and then we all go into Cape Town to do the necessary. If we all go down to Cape Town in December Audrey and I will want at least two clear days to do some personally shopping (clothes, as we haven't bought anything up to now) Think it over and let us know. If you and Marius have anything you want us to do please let me know and we'll get cracking. I have already assumed that you will both want knitted caps, any particular colours wanted!!!

1. CLOTHES. By the sounds of things you intend to keep Audrey & I up to scratch!! Anyway many thanks for allowing us a bit more clothing. What size case do you suggest - we both have a choice as far as size goes - you will know how best they will pack. Kaht do you think to a sort of hanging bag - we thought your two suites and our better dresses could hang in a dust-proof bag. You talk of smart clothes, by that I take it as something semi-evening, to wear when you chaps wear a suite. We are a bit worried as to what kind of shoes to take. What do you thing to something in th line of canvass (fulled covering the foot) for Africa during the day, we could wear socks with same, a pair of sandels for town wear, a pair of strong leather shoes and a pair for dancing. See how lucky you fellows are - one pair will do for you. Don't worry about the weight we will keep it down as much as possible.
2. ROUTE. As far as we are concerned any way will do. Up the East Coast sounds terrific. Audrey has not seen the Falls and did want to but she says she doesn't mind all that much. We feel that you know more about the routes than we do so you just go ahead - we're right with you. We take it that we must get Visas for all the African Territories just in case we have to change our Route. How are we coming back? or do we discuss this later. We are quite easy either way.

- 2 -

3. Y.H.A. Yes I'll get your cards but you will have to send me some passport photos. We could also get your Visas when and if we go to Cape Town but we will need your Passports. We will both get International Driving Permits - Audrey already has a valid one. By the way are you and Marius going home to Ceres before we leave. What do your parents think of this trip?

4. Food DEPARTMENT. We agree that each one should get his own plate cup knife fork and spoon. Audrey and I will provide the extras from our homes. We will also get an extra pan, pot and basin. Just leave this until you come down to pick us up and then you can pick out what will be most useful and the rest can stay behind. As far as actual food goes we thought we could live off the land as much as possible as be go along. For the time when we can't get food we can carry such things as powdered egg, dried fruit, powdered milk, pkts of soup, boerebiskuit and biltong. We have tried to tink of all the things that won't weigh too much but all seem to need water. How will we carry water? What sort of primus do you advocate - the ordinary one or a box one? We have an ordinary one, which we can take. What about a lamp?
5. ADVERTISING. I am enclosing a letter from a friend who works for Vacuum Oil Co. - it explains itself. Anyway we won't give up Audrey is going to write to Shell Overseas and we will try any other firm for anything - maybe we will be lucky. Audrey is also going to try and sell our story. I do hope that the Volkswagen factory will come to light.
6. DIE SKILPAD. You silly so and so why didn't you tell us what colour our travelling home is. Here we are dying to know something about it and all you tell us is its milage and touring vacalities. Gosh Carel you really sound as if you have struck something wonderful. We will be travelling in style. Where on earth did you find such a Kombi. Audrey says she will paint the Union flag on the front but she wants to know how much window space there is - from the point of view as to how much space she will have for sign-writing. Also what colour do you suggest she does her sign-writing?
7. WEAPONS. I have a gas pistol, do you think I should take it? Audrey and I are going to the Police for lessons on how to use a pistol but we do not intend buying one - we'll use yours if necessary.
8. MEDICAL. Yes I'll fix up a box and get plenty of Paludrine.
9. SLEEPING. Audrey and I think that Marius should also get us sleeping-bags. They will be far easies to pack us etc. Please let us know how much they will cost and we will send some money up. Are you two going to sleep on the ground? Have you thought of strechers or those blow-up mattress. I have sheet sleeping bags for all of us - the Youth Hostel kind.

10. We can also supply a piece of canvase 6 x 7, cushions and pillows (if wanted) a rug. Carel if you think of anything that we may have please write and we will add it to our list. After all it we have got it why buy.

11. PHOTOGRAPHY. Have either of you got a 35 mm camera for colour film. Bunny Joseph suggested that we take such a camera and keep it for colour films. What do you think? Also what do you suggest we do about this matter. Audrey has a very good Zeiss (cost appro. £60.) which takes 120 film and mine is an Agfa Isolette also taking 120 film.

12. LUGGAGE. Carel as I explained to you previously Audrey and I had planned to work in England so we will need more clothing than we will be taking in the Kombi. We have the clothing so we do not see the point in buying other clothing Overseas. We want to ship some extra clothing to England to Audrey's Uncle at Torquay. We believe that Parry Leon & Hayhoe do this sort of thing - seeing it through the Customs both ends etc. What do you think, would you like to send something with our stuff? This is one of the things we want to fix up in Cape Town if we go down in October.

Well that is all for now- sorry to give you such a headache! By the way if you want any typing done just send it down - mind you not that I am a first class typist but at least I can manage more than one finger.

p.s. Marius and I will get our visas in Pretoria.
We can get yours too if you want.

Box 99,
Klerksdorp,
24 th Sept. 1957.

Hullo Joan and Aubry,

I hav e progressed so far that I type now with two fingers. Please excuse all faults, typing, spelling and otherwise.

First I'll discuss business and then we'll chat. I'll answer your letter point for point as you wrote it.

1) Clothes: How is it that you dont mention dresses in your first list?. It is just shorts, jeans and slacks. WE might mistake you later for two men. 'Alle grappies op 'n stokie', I do think you should consentrate a bit more on a few dresses. For Africa a kaki skirt and shirt and for Europe anny thing you like.. There traveling is very clean and we will be most of the times in towns. You did not know I had such old fasioned ideas, did you? In any case here is a short list of what I recon you should take. Consider it as a recommendation onely, 1 pair slacks, 1pr. jeans(?), 2pr. shorts, 2cotton shirts, 2long sleeved blouses and 2 short sleeved ones, 2 jerseys, light rain coat, and a coat, 2 pajamas, undies, bathing suit and dresses for town wear. Your list for shoes I find O. K.

There is no place in the Kombi to hang a hanging bag for clothes, unless we hang it in front of one of the windows. So I suggest takinga big suitcase for all our good clothes. I have one 2 ft. x 1 ft. 9 inch. x 9 inch. If you have a better one we can take that. W.D.M.G. (i.e. will discus this matter when we reach George.)

2) Route and Visas: At present it will onely be neccessary to get visas for Egipt(20 Feb. to 4 March 1958) and maybe Itally (March, entering at Brindesi leaving through Bremer pass or to France.) Visas for Sudan and Ethiopie we get in Nairobi. The visas for Europe I prefer to get in Europe. One can then get them for the correct period one will spend in the country.

Have you British or South African passports?.

Will you get us the adresses of the British Consulates along our route, I'll get the South Africa ones. We South Africans are also entitled to go to the British Consule.

When we reach Egipt and if the Kombi and our Finance are still good we can Go to Turky and from there to Greece, Yugoslavia and EUrope another reason to wait in getting visas.

~~4) Y.H.A. THANKS, we'll send our photo's~~

4) Food etc. as you said in your letter W.D.M.G. No lamps required but it will be usefull if each has his own torch, the smaller the better.

5) Advertising: Super Sonic Radio's has promised us their strongest radio set on the market, free of charge. Have not heard from Volks Wagen yet.

6) Die Skilpad alias the Flying Bedstead; Do'nt you know that at present the Kombi is the onely car you can chose which couler you want---- as long as you chose BLUE. Aubry if you insist on painting the windows I'll insist on driving all the wayso I can see the senery. Why not paint on the car itself?.

7) It may be good if you take the gas pistol with,---- you may need it to keep the Marais'es in their place.

9) Sl-eping-bags, we'll discuss later.

10) W.D.M.G.

11)Photography: At the moment I am trying out a coulerfilm in my camera. If it is no good we'll have to buy a 35 milimeter camera. We all have very good cameras which should be good enough for couler photography. I think we should also get a movie, a KODAK one costs onely £15 or with three extra lenses £34 . What will be most usefull will be a pair of binoculars, cant you borrow one some where?.

12) Thanks for the offer about the luggage. At present we cant do anny thing about it. If you can wait till December we'll have something to send with, but if it is inconvenient for you to wait then dont wait.

About your first query, it may be best if you go to Cape Town in October if necessary we go down again in December.

Thanks for the ofer of the cape. You chose the coulere.

You two may still be kicked out of the Flying Bedstead to sleep in the tent becaus there is a great possibility that Johan may go with. So you will be swamped by the Marais. I hope you wont object to Johan going with, if you do then lodge your complaints at my address.

We hope to come down to George about 5th. December, then to Ceres and Cape Town

I think I'll cut the chatting out becaus I am in a bad mood. Someone pinched £5 off me today and it still hurts, so I feel more like crying on your shoulders than chatting, so please excuse me for being short and businesslike.

Au REVOIR fellow globe trotters,

Carl.

P.O. BOX 11,
GEORGE, C.P.
4th October, 1957.

Dear Carel,

Many thanks for your letter, we loved your sense of humour. Mind you I must just add that you chaps will probably get quite mad at Audrey and me because we have such highly developed senses of humour. So don't complain at a later date that you weren't fore-warned. This letter writing business is getting quite a business - I spent 11 hours writing letters last week-end. I suppose that is the worst of having so many curious friends - still I like writing (if I can spare the time) so I must not grouse. I'll answer your letter point for point and then add a few queries, so here goes:-

1. Clothes. Sorry to have caused you worry!!!! I know our first list was very limited but then we thought that we were only going to be allowed a little space and weight. We were just taking the barest amount but now that you say space is no object (but still trying to keep the weight down) we have added quite a considerable amount of "Ladies attire". I don't think there will be any danger of you chaps mistaking us for two fellows!!! But you must also bear in mind that our not being able to iron does make a difference to what we can take. Anyway we will sort ourselves out and I'm sure you will feel very proud of us when we all go out together. By the way have you chaps managed to get light rain-coats yet? Audrey and I managed to get two lovely American Plastic ones, which fold up into quite a small parcel.

2. Route & Visas. From your letter I take it that we only need get Visas for Portuguese East Africa, Kenya and Egypt (20 Feb. to 20 March 1958). Audrey has a British Passport and I have a South African passport. We will get all the addresses of the British Consulates along out route.

3. Advertising. What wonderful new about Super Sonic Radio. It's a funny thing but Audrey and I were wondering whether a radio would be a useful thing before we heard whether the Kombi had one or not. We are keeping out fingers crossed in the hope that Volkswagen will come to light. It will mean so much to us and I'm sure to them as well. By the way I think your W.D.M.G. very clever - I can see our latter letters reading like this - 1. W.D.M.G., 2. W.D.M.G., 6. W.D.M.G.!!!!!

4. Photography. Carel it is all very well trying Colour film in your camera - we wanted to try colour film in ours as well but it really doesn't help much because it will be difficult trying to find a universal projected to show them. The 35 millimeter is the common one that's why Audrey and I gave up the idea of using colour in our cameras.

But don't buy a 35 milimeter camera until you hear from me again. Thel. and Rodney are wanting to give me something and I have asked them for one which I hope I will get within a week or two. If they decide against it I'll let you know (in time). Audrey has a set of developing equipment and in the past has done a lot of developing for herself. She wants to know whether you think she should take it along and develope our films as and when we come to plenty of water. At present we are both making experiments with Kodak Verichrome Pan films which Audrey is going to develope. I will let you know what results we have. Mr. Goldie and Mr. Jolly have given us quite a bit of advice so we are hoping for results. Photography can be really exasperating one time you have some success and think you are really good and then the very next film you spoil, I suppose it's all in the game. So far we have not managed to get a pair of binoculars but we haven't given up yet.

5. Luggage. Carel we are not quite sure yet when Parry Leon and Hayhoe will want our luggage for shipping but we will work it so that you chaps will be able to include something with our stuff. This is one of the things we want to get straightened out in Cape Town when we go down in October (gosh I only realise now that it is this month, time is catching up on us) I will write later what Parry Leon & Hayhoe have to say on the subject.

6. Travelling Companions. I am so pleased that Johan doesn't think we are sor made that he is now considering to join up with us. Do you know what Audrey and I said as soon as we read your letter "This will cut down our expenses". Funny how conscious one becomes of money when not having much and planning a trip like ours. Please tell Johan from us that we don't mind in the least or should be say not until something trys to eat us while we sleep in the tent - then I can see the 3 Marais's being pulled out of bed & hurled into the tent for the rest of the trip!!!! By the way you didn't say what you & Marius have to think. Also what does Johan's girl-friend think?

Carel one other small point that has puzzled Audrey and me. You talked about going to night-clubs etc., does Marius dance?(& Johan for that matter too) We know you love dancing and so do we but how do the others feel about it. You should be like me, I never carry much money around on me - therefore if would be no good anyone trying to pinch from me. Mind you I can sympathise with you, makes one feel as if people have no respect for you. Well Carel this will be all for now - regards to our fellow-globe trotters.

Have extra keys cut

P.O. BOX 99,
Klerksdorp.
30 th. October 1957.

Hullo Joan and Aubry,

Please excuse me for taking such a long time in answering your last letter. The trouble was a dark and despondend mood and when I am in such a mood I just sleep and do nothing else.

What have you got against hitting the headlines?, it makes one feel important.

Joan you onely now starts to think that you'll have to do some work, it does me great pleasure to disillusion you; who do you think will make the coffie in the morning, whois going to wash the Kombi(and it is a great area to wash), who is going to write our daily log etc. You and Aubry will need an holliday after Marius and I have finished with you two, that is if we succeed in making you darn our socks wash our clothes and do our private correspondence too (maybe I am a bit optimistic and we might have to do a few of these items ourselves------ if not all of them). In anny case I'll like to take the type writer with if possible. I prefer typing with the one finger to writing (that is if our pr ofessional typist is not available.

Now business, and bad news to start with. Volkswagen does not want to know our troubles,--- thats that. Secondly the Sudan wants a £100 guarentee per person before giving us a permit. Last time Adriaan and I went to their border and said were we are with no deposito what now, so they let us through. We can try that again otherwise it is the Sahara for us. The comming weekend I am going to see a fellow who's done that trip, I'll let you know what he say.

The Super Sonic Company wants us to go through Bulawayo because their factory is there. From there we can still go through Nyasaland etc.

About the visas, I think it best to wri te now and get the application forms, get them for Belgium Congo, French West Africa, and Egipt. We'll have enough time in December, but getting the forms now will save time then.

The Marais (plural) will have also to get jobs in Europe, I want to try England first, about the others I dont know.

Actually I think it does not matter what travellers cheque s we take. Most probably Marius and myself will have Cooks travellers cheques, so it may be good if you take Barclays and/or Standerd Bank travellers cheques. How much money to take with?, that is a difficult question, why not take all with as travellers cheques or is that uneconomical? I think you should atleast take £150 each in travellers cheques for the tour, that is to play safe. About Egipt it now is not sure weather we'll go through there or not , so we wait with that problem of money exchange there.

My experiments with couler film was a success, they were excelent. One do get projectors for these films, I have seen one in Joburg for £19, suitable for projecting 2¼ by 2¼ and 35 milimeter films. the onely trouble is that my films costs 1/- per photo more than a 35 milimeter film.

Weather you takeyour developing equipment wither or not I leave to you to decide, but remember W.S (weight and space). If you want me to air my opinion I'll say wait;W.D.M.G., for then we can see what extras we can include.

My parents are kicking very much against my going..They say I am waisting my time galovating (hope that spelling is correct) around onthis earth of ours. They dont mind the others so much. Since the previous sentence two days have gon by and in the mean time I received a letter from my parents; they dont squeel so much anny more.

How are we going to organise the big "AFFAIRT"? I expect that we will be in George about 10 th. Dec.(maybe sooner or later), then we make final arrangements and then we Marais must go to Ceres for a week or so. Would you like to go with to Ceres?,my parents will appreciate it if you will spend afew days there so they can learn to know you. From Ceres we can go to Cape Town for visas etc. and for the takeoff. There is no need to decide now, but just think about it.

Have you two though how you are going to sleep in the tent,,atleast on what are you going to sleep?. I have more or less solved it but may be you have better ideas than me, at least cheaper, remember again W. S. & C. (weight, space & cost); this is wrong it should be W.S.T.&C. ,you puzzel yourseves out what that last T. stands for.

Now, I think this is enough for a three day effort,so I'll end with the famous words of Confucious. "Hou die blinkkant bo, en as dit 'n bietjie roes draai dit dan net om!"

Au Revoir.

Corel.

Map of the Route Travelled

ALL SET for GREAT TRANS-AFRICA TRIP

(Wilderness Correspondent)

A great adventure will shortly begin for Miss Audrey Nives of Sands Road, the Wilderness, and Miss Joan Povall of George. In company with Mr. Carel and Mr. Marius Marais of Ceres, C.P., and travelling by a Volkswagon kombi, they intend to to cross the Continents of Africa and Europe with London as their final destination.

Miss Nives has for some time intended to return to England, where she was born, for a visit, and she and Miss Povall had already planned a trip by sea when they were invited by Mr. Carel Marais to undertake this more adventurous journey.

This will be the first trip abroad for Miss Povall, but Mr. Carel Marais has already successfully completed this journey to London before, in three and a half months.

SEND-OFF

Departure at this time of year has been recommended by a motor association to avoid the worst rains in Central and North Africa. Departure from Cape Town, with an official send-off, has been scheduled for December 21st.

The exact route to be followed will depend largely on the political situation in the Middle East, and on the granting of numerous visas and entry permits necessary for several countries en route.

No attempt is to be made to break any records, and the party intend to spend several days in as many places of interest as possible.

All are International Members of the Youth Hostel Association, and if possible use will be made of any Youth Hostels en route, although priority facilities are usually granted to hikers and cyclists.

THE ROUTE

The proposed route is from Cape Town to the Victoria Falls via Bulawayo, through Tanganyika and Kenya to Nairobi and then directly north to Addis Ababa.

Continuing through Ethiopia they will proceed to Khartoum in the Sudan, where they hope to board a Nile steamer, which will take them down the Nile to Cairo. From Alexandria they will cross the Mediterranean into Turkey calling at Ankara and Istanbul, then proceed to cross Europe via Greece, Yugoslavia, Austria and Germany, finally arriving in London some time in April.

IN LONDON

Upon their arrival in London, they will probably remain there for a while, then return to Europe during the summer to tour other countries not previously visited.

Miss Nives plans to remain in London for some time afterwards, taking a job as an architect's assistant.

Many months of detailed planning and hard work have been put into her preparations for the trip. The Kombi is already fitted for touring with twin bunks and additional sleeping accommodation is provided by a lean-to tent. With a weight and space limit to consider, priority has been given to the carrying of water, petrol and paraffin, and a complete set of spare engine parts, tyres and electrical equipment needed.

LIGHT WEIGHT

Wishing to be as independent as possible, their food supplies will consist mainly of tinned and packeted goods, powdered milk and eggs. Considerable use is to be made of lightweight plastic containers.

Medical supplies against tropical fevers, minor illnesses and injuries have also to be carried. Clothing has been strictly limited to lightweight tropical clothing, with a small amount of warmer clothing against a European winter and spring.

PICTURES

A movie camera and films have been donated by a well-known photographic firm, and a Cape Town electrical firm are supplying a radio receiver with which the party have been requested to keep a daily log on radio reception.

Miss Nives, who works as an architectural draughtswoman in George, greatly admires Egyptian sculpture and architecture, and hopes to find much to interest her while in Egypt.

WILD LIFE

She is also looking forward to making a study of African wild life in which she also has a great interest. All members of the party are very fond of outdoor life and camping and have no apprehensions about their venture.

A newspaper clipping from 1957 reporting on the planned trip

The Diary Entries

Dec 20: Joan and Audrey posing with the Kombi in Cape Town. Table Mountain in the background

Sunday, 29th December 1957

Today I left home to start this wonderfully exciting road trip to London. Carel, Audrey, Marius and I, left George at 6:30 am. Mum was very sad and so was I. She has been so wonderful. Thel and Rod[1] could not say much. We travelled all day and night through the Cape, Orange Free State and entered the Transvaal. It rained all the way which made for very pleasant travelling.

Leaving George, Western Cape

Monday, 30th December 1957

Arrived at Klerksdorp at 3:35 am. Parked the Kombi alongside the Vaal River and slept until daylight. Had breakfast then Carel left with the Kombi to get it serviced while Audrey, Marius and I went to the swimming bath. Carel did some business and then joined us. It was wonderful swimming as it was so very hot. Carel did some diving which I photographed. We spent the late afternoon in the park. Went to a farewell party at the Town Engineer's office, it was most enjoyable. Met Johan for the first time, he came out from another party. We slept

---

1 *Thel is Joan's younger sister, Rod her fiancé.*

in a flat, belonging to a friend of Carel's, at Vanderbyl Park. It was very comfortable.

Carel diving

Tuesday, 31st December 1957

Up very early after a good sleep. The boys arrived late 8:10 am after sleeping in the Kombi down by the river. Did some washing then left for Johannesburg. Marius and Audrey took the Kombi over to Pretoria to get Audrey's Egyptian visa and fix Johan's passport. Carel and I spent the day in Joburg shopping for last minute bits and pieces for the trip. He took me into an Italian street café, thoroughly enjoyed it. We then went to Supersonic for our farewell and had tea with Mr Ivan Baris of Keystone Cameras. Took a lot of cine photos at Supersonic, it was a lovely farewell. Went to Johan's flat in Sasolburg for supper and to complete some paperwork for the tour, helped pack up. We then started the New Year by being fetched from the flat to go to a party. What a jolly party! Mostly Germans who were technicians from the factory. We danced until 2:30 am. We decided that if we wanted to start early, we should better turn in. Slept in the flat at Vanderbyl Park, Carel and Marius slept in the Kombi again.

Wednesday, 1st January 1958 (Daraprim Taken)

The boys came to breakfast after which they went to pack Johan into the Kombi and Audrey and I did some washing, ironing and letter writing. The flat has been a real Godsend, we are all clean again, clothes and personally. The boys arrived back at 1 pm and we went and had New Year's dinner at a Roadhouse– mixed grill. We all enjoyed lunch as we hadn't had a heavy meal for days – cost us £1–10–9. Started our tour with lunch in Pretoria. Had tea with Tielman and family then later met Willem's family as well, we had supper there[2]. Said our goodbyes and travelled about 10 miles out of Pretoria and set up our 1st camp[3]. Went to bed as it was 10 pm by then, very comfortable. We were all a bit quiet as if feeling our way. I was very tired.

Thursday, 2nd January 1958

Had a really good night's sleep, awoke full of beans. We got away to a good start and got on to the road at 7:45 am. Mind you Carel wants us to improve on that, we must be on the road by 7 am. We took 1½-hour turns at the wheel and travelled until 5 pm. The countryside in the Northern Transvaal looks beautiful, they have had rain and the bushveld is very green. Travelled through Nylstroom, Potgieter's Rust, Pietersburg, crossed the Tropic of Capricorn and into Louis Trichardt. I saw ostrich about five miles on the southern side of Louis Trichardt, we were very surprised to see them so far north. We were also struck by the very big anthills south of Potgieter's Rust. The native huts are of the mud and plaited reed roof type, very picturesque all set against the side of the mountains. Louis Trichardt is surrounded by a lot of forests and the view from the pass on the north side is breath-taking. Struck camp 10 miles north of Louis Trichardt. I did supper while Audrey painted. Carel and I fetched water from the river and saw some

---

2 *Tielman and Willem Marais are the older brothers of Johan, Carel and Marius.*

3 *Johan brought along a blow up mattress which was punctured by a thorn this first night and had to be thrown away. The others had a good giggle at his intended luxury that did not last the first night!*

monkeys. It rained while we ate and we all huddled under the tent. To bed and wrote letters.

Audrey crossing the Tropic of Capricorn.

Friday, 3rd January 1958 (My Birthday, 26 Years)

It rained hard during the night, the tent collapsed but the boys managed to fix it. Marius dug a trench around the tent and Kombi to stop the boys getting washed away. Woke up with birthday greetings from Carel. Each one gave me a penny as a birthday present, a very sweet thought. Ate birthday cake after we had passed through the SA Customs at Beitbridge. It rained all morning. I drove over Beitbridge at 11:55 am and into Rhodesia. Had some fun with the customs officials over the number of cameras, guns and binoculars we were carrying. Carel took some cine film of us at the customs. The cyclone "Aspedid" was catching up with us, very heavy rain. We ran out of the rain just after 2 pm. Camped down at Gwanda after travelling approximately 140 miles, not much as we had started late due to the rain. I did all our washing while the boys pitched camp and Audrey did some signwriting on the Kombi. Supper was a tin of marmalade and bread with table wine, my health was drunk. Also had some prickly pear which was very nice. A very nice birthday indeed. Carel said I was a special girl so I was let off my jobs.

Saturday, 4th January 1958

It started raining at 4 am. Cyclone Aspedid had caught up with us again. It just came down in buckets, the boys were completely swamped out in the outside tent so we packed up and were on the road by 5 am. Everything was wet, sleeping bags, pillows, blankets and some clothes. Stopped to wash and dress in decent clothes, the boys were still in swim trunks, five miles out of Bulawayo[4]. Carel went to see Supersonic while we did some shopping. It stopped raining 50 miles north of Bulawayo so we struck camp at 2:10 pm to dry out our things. I washed and cooked, Audrey painted[5], Carel did the books and Johan and Marius serviced the Kombi. Bed early to write letters. We were all proud of the Kombi over her performance in the rain. Our first dry night of the trip.

Drying gear

---

[4] *The newspaper that day reported 8 inch of rain in the area they had travelled through the previous day. The roads behind them had been closed.*

[5] *Audrey, an accomplished artist, completed a painting of an African hut pulling a smaller one to symbolize the travelling home with a travelling toilet in tow. She painted above in Xhosa the words "Ikaya eli Hambaya" which translates to "the house that travels". It can also however have a more symbolic meaning of "home is a journey". It is for this later meaning and what it symbolized that I named this book*

Cooking, painting and car care

Sunday, 5th January 1958

Up very early – I seem to be the first one up always. Travelled all day through elephant country, but didn't see any. Saw our first monkeys and baboons. Stopped at Waai Bridge filling station to wash, our water ran out the night before. Some lovely elephant skulls as the gateposts. Drove on to Wankie – the boys wanted a drink but the bars were still closed. Arrived at Victoria Falls at 5:20 pm. Found a terrific camp spot right near the bathrooms. After supper we saw the Falls by moonlight. It was a beautiful sight.

Monday, 6th January 1958

Woke very early at 5:50 am. Got up and did all our washing which had been soaking all night. Carel was also up early writing up his books. After breakfast we started doing the Falls from the Northern Bank, lovely views with rainbows caught in the mist. I was very hot. As we reached the bridge it started raining, carried on all day. We got soaking wet. I was the only one with a mac on. Audrey had a short jacket on and she got very wet. The poor boys didn't even have jackets on. Carel, Audrey and I walked through the rain forest. It was good fun as there was plenty of rain, the Zambezi was very full. Had tea and scones on the South Bank where the taxi picked us up for a boat ride. What a taxi driver, a native boy driving a clapped-out Vauxhall, how we flew along. It was quite frightening, anyway we got there safely. Went out in a small boat with a 35 hp outboard motor. She went like a bomb. Had tea on Palm Island, just the five of us and the driver. Saw a lot of hippos. Coming back it poured with rain, we all got soaked for the umpteenth time. Back to camp for showers, eat, bed and letter writing.

Off on the boat trip of the Falls

Falls

Tuesday, 7th January 1958

Well what do you know, Carel got up early and gave us breakfast in bed, quite a treat. Wrote letters in bed after breakfast. Johan and Marius greased the car, it took them until 11:30 am. Audrey and I cleaned up quite a bit and wrote letters. I was a bit down hearted; Audrey and I can't work together; it is a pity because team-work is always much quicker. I am sorry about this especially after the way Sue and I worked together. Left Victoria Falls just after 12 pm. Still had a lot of wet washing, I do wish we could run out of the rain. It is beginning to get me down. We drove along the Hubert Young Drive and looked at the 3rd and 4th Gorges. What a long way down to the river. Arrived at Livingstone just as the shops shut for lunch hour so we had to wait to buy food. Had a look at the museum, a wonderful show of Livingstone's travelling equipment and letters. Met a gentleman who advised us not to go to Salisbury thereby avoiding the rain belt. He advised that we keep to the Great North Road. So we changed our route which will mean no post in Salisbury. I will miss it, we won't get mail now until we get to Dar es Salaam. Camped for the night about 60 miles north of Livingstone.

Wednesday, 8th January 1958 (Take Daraprim)

Up very early 5 am – had a good wash and then got breakfast. We were on the road by 7:15 am, our earliest so far. A good day travelling on the Great North Road through Zimba, Choma, Pemba where we posted some letters at a post office run by Africans. They were very interested in our trip, seemed very educated. On through Monze where there is a very big maize depot, very big buildings. Through Mazabuka where we bought bread 1/3p a white loaf, eggs 5/- a dozen. Travelled over the Kafue River, there was a roadblock there trying to catch some fellow who had pinched a car in Salisbury. Bought meat in Kafue and then left for Kariba. Camped down early as we had to be up early tomorrow to see Kariba. Audrey and I had a good wash down before going to bed, it was wonderful. We all got into bed and under our mosquito nets and spent an hour or more talking, letter writing then off to sleep. The scenery today was beautiful, hilly and very green with more thorn trees. A wonderful day.

Thursday, 9th January 1958 (Sue's Birthday)

Camped down for the night about 15 miles out of Kafue on the Kariba road. Up early and on the road to Kariba. Arrived at the barrier at 9:15, but were not allowed in. Carel took a lift with a tractor mechanic to fetch us an entry permit from the South Bank barrier. We four sat in the Kombi writing letters. Carel arrived back 1½ hours later with two fellows, who were giving him a lift back as his request had been refused, but they suddenly had a change of heart. Alex Kyle and Percy Jacobson, they were very good to us and showed us all over Kariba. What a tremendous engineering feat. It was very hard to believe. We spent two hours looking around and then they took us to their home for a beer and lunch, all cooked by the boy, the servants do everything for them. How we enjoyed our first sit down meal for over two weeks, we even managed to have a good wash. We were very lucky to see Kariba and we only saw it because Percy gave Carel a lift inside the construction area[6]. Kariba was at the end cofferdam stage, the Zambezi was very full. Saw the dam site all covered with trees and bush – 200 miles long and 30 miles wide. Camped north of Kafue very tired, terrorised by mosquitoes and horseflies. A wonderful day, one I shall always remember.

Dam construction

[6] *My dad had entered a restricted/no trespassers zone of the dam where permits were required to enter the construction site. Although his request to enter had been refused, he was hoping he would be granted one on the basis of being a fellow civil engineer. This was not the case and he maintains that it was only when the girls (Joan and Audrey) came into the picture that the change of heart happened and thereafter they got VIP treatment.*

Exploring construction of the dam.

Friday, 10th January 1958

Up very early as we wanted to do over 250 miles. Arrived in Lusaka at 10:10 am. A very modern city with very wide streets. Posted letters did some shopping, bought wool for a jersey for Rod. The boys were very patient while Audrey and I shopped. It is still raining every afternoon. Had afternoon tea at Broken Hill. Also a very good neat town with very modern houses. Met the manager of a Manganese mine who was very interested in our tour, he asked us out to the mine for supper, we didn't go as I was too far for us to travel. Left Broken Hill for Kapiri Mposhi. Camped down in the middle of a quarry about 15 miles south of Kapiri. Pleasantly cool, had a good supper, no mosquitoes so we crammed into the Kombi and talked until just after 10 pm. The first social evening we have had and I think we all enjoyed the change from letter writing, reading and bed. Johan is at last coming into his own, he has a very keen sense of humour. Marius also seems to be mellowing. Carel of course is always full of fun. We all went to bed after tea. very content.

Saturday, 11th January 1958

It rained during the night so we didn't get up very early. If I am late then no one else wakes and gets up early. Even Carel overslept. Travelled to Kapiri, a small trading station. Bought mangoes at 2 for 1d, delicious. The countryside has not changed much for the last three days. The roads are not so good, very muddy which has slowed down our speed considerably. Rained again so we are all getting a bit tired of the wet but we should run out of it in a day or two once we get into Tanganyika. Carel was in a bad mood today, it matched mine completely. Audrey was very tired. Camped down near Mpika after going just on 250 miles today.

Sunday, 12th January 1958

Up late – the boys serviced the car so we didn't get on the road until after 9 am. Audrey and I did some washing. The scenery changed, did a lot of climbing, could see a sea of green every time we reached a hilltop. Very lonely road, only passed three cars, ran out of petrol, turned over to the reserve tank and got to Chinsali. Went into the Govt Commissioner House for petrol, to be supplied tomorrow. Spent the night at the Chinsali Govt Rest House, the boys slept inside, Audrey and I in the Kombi. Had hot baths, wrote letters in the lounge. Very comfortable indeed. Picked my first mangoes at the Commissioner's House.

Chinsali house

Monday, 13th January 1958

Slept late, it was wonderful. Johan brought us early morning tea. Then wonder of wonders Carel gave Audrey and I breakfast in bed. We felt very spoilt indeed. Johan went down to the Govt Office at Chinsali for petrol while we cleaned up. Wrote letters and did some washing. Travelled from Chinsali to Isoka off the main road. Beautiful forest country, saw a herd of small bucks. Very hot, travelled through a very heavy thunderstorm, at times we could hardly see through the windows. Carel and I sat at the back had a very serious talk all about why we five were travelling together, our fate. I wouldn't tell him why I thought the two of us were travelling together, but I think he knows as well as I do. We have to finish off this talk at a later date, too soon to say anything now. I only hope we both stick it out until we get to London. From then on anything can happen. Camped down 10 miles south of Tunduma. I felt bilious, couldn't get sick though. Lovely evening, Carel and I went for a walk, to bed, early to sleep.

Muddy car

Muddy roads

Tuesday, 14th January 1958

Broke camp early, had no bread but Audrey fried four eggs we got from a native girl, I didn't want mine. Tunduma turned out to be a native village with a few stores. Crossed the border at Vwawa and on into Tanganyika. Went through customs at Vwawa, dealt with by an Indian Customs Official and African Police boys, all very smart. Travelled through the Tanganyika highlands' wonderful scenery, I could see for about 20 miles around from the mountain tops. Climbed 2000 feet in the distance of five miles. Wonderful native settlements. Reached Mbeya at 11:30 am. Went through the immigration office at the Mbeya police office. All Africans were very smart and polite. There was also an Indian officer who was, very smart and dignified. Bought provisions. Carel, Audrey and I walked around the native bazaar, very interesting and most colourful. Our first day without rain, very hot but we all enjoyed the change. Camped down north of Chimala, got petrol from the hotel. Water from the river, first time we are using river water. Bed early, plenty of mosquitoes. A wonderful scenic day, enjoyed it.

Wednesday, 15th January 1958 (Take Daraprim)

Couldn't break camp too early on account of the mosquitoes. Johan and Carel serviced the Kombi. Didn't sleep too well so I was sleepy just about all day. Slept in the morning. The roads are bad, hard with plenty of potholes. The Kombi is really taking a hammering. We have had to slow our speed to save too much bumping. Travelled through very mountainous country, no rain. Arrived at Iringa at 3:30 pm to find the bank closed. Decided to camp outside Iringa and come again in the morning to draw money. Iringa is built on top of a mountain overlooking a river valley – the river meanders along, very green countryside and very picturesque. Found a very nice camp spot. Audrey and I did our washing. No flies or mosquitoes, heavenly, so we stayed up quite late. Beautiful sunset while we ate supper. We all had a hot wash down using the plastic basin which, after a dusty day, was utter bliss. Audrey had a headache. Carel and I went for a walk down by the river. There were hundreds of fireflies. The sky was very clear and the stars beautiful.

Thursday, 16th January 1958

We slept late because we only had to be at the bank after 9 am. Used Barclays Bank Iringa, it is run completely by Indians except for the accountant and manager. Did some shopping. Left Iringa at 10:30 am. Travelled from Iringa, over the escarpment to within 20 miles of Morogoro. The road winds in and out, round hairpin bends, over bridges, up and down and over the Ruapa River. Very beautiful countryside with plenty of baobab trees in one section. This river is very wide in spots and very muddy in colour. Saw plenty of baboons on the riverbanks and a herd of buck. Expected to see crocs and hippos but our luck was out. Saw elephant droppings on the road but no elephant. The road was shockingly corrugated and dusty. The poor Kombi will need a new set of shock absorbers at this rate. The native huts have changed again. These are built entirely of bamboo and reeds and are very neat. The Africans in these parts wear long nightshirts type of garments and all the men carry big black umbrellas. They look comical, they use them as sunshades or umbrellas. Their women seem to do all the work from the ploughing to bringing up children. Camped and then sat outside talking until 11 pm. Enjoyed ourselves due to no mosquitoes. Travelled over the Kitonga Pass.

Boabab trees

Photo stop

Friday, 17th January 1958

Up early and travelled into Morogoro. A very big city but very dirty. Walked around the market. What a collection – anything from food to hardware, very interesting though. Travelled on to Dar es Salaam, it was very hot. Good tarred road for a change. Arrived in Dar just after 3 pm. It was cooking hot. Went to the Visitors Bureau and then the police to see about a camping spot. Drove along the beach front and found a camping spot at Oyster Bay beneath the waving palms. Had a swim, it was really worth all the heat and stickiness of the four days prior. The water was warm and we swam just beyond the coral reef. A really wonderful spot for swimming. I got my first letters from home, how I enjoyed reading on the beach. Decided to go for a drink so Audrey and I had to put on dresses. Went to a place called Ocean Breeze which is built right on the seafront. We all had beers and beer shandy, they were terrific. We found a swing big enough to take all five of us, what fun. Pitched camp in the dark, had supper and then sat under the palm trees in the breeze. Carel picked some coconuts for us.

Joan

Saturday, 18th January 1958

Couldn't sleep very well, too hot. Got up early and sat on the beach in my pyjamas until it was almost light. Then put on my costume and went for a swim. Carel joined me and we walked all along the beach of Oyster Bay. Watched the sun rise, it was very beautiful coming over the sea. Picked some coconuts, they were delicious. Had a late breakfast and then went into town to get some provisions. Carel and I walked around together, we had fun at the curio shops. He says he is going to watch my money for me. Went to Msasani Beach for a swim. The water was about 75°F, but much deeper than at Oyster Bay. We went and looked at the harbour, there were not many ships in dock. Motored to the African market. What a crowd, they seem to sell everything there. Plenty of fruit, we bought some very big mangoes, the size of paw-paws. They were terrific, the best flavoured ones I have ever eaten. The fish and meat stalls at the market were absolutely revolting. Enough to put you off both for life. Pitched camp at Oyster Bay, supper. Went to bio to see "Picnic", just a lot of rubbish. Carel and I spent just about all the time talking. Mind you a very nice air-conditioned cinema. No colour, but plenty of Indian men in bio. Back at camp Carel made tea and then we all turned in as we were tired. Marius had an earache.

Carel looking out over the Bay

Sunday, 19th January 1958

Slept very well, up early to see the sunrise and to have a swim. Carel also came down onto the beach early. Took some cine films of him picking coconuts. While we were having breakfast Carel found a water main very near our camp. He opened it up and we had water on tap. It was simply marvellous. Audrey and I did all our dirty washing, what a job it took us from 10 am to 3 pm. Anyway we had a good time as we were able to shower each other down when we got too hot. While Carel and I were swimming earlier he had his watch pinched out of the Kombi. The boys went into town to see the police[7] and to fix up our trip to Zanzibar. Had a hair wash, wrote letters. Had supper then Carel and I walked along the beach, it was heavenly, after the heat of the day. Mind you I think we are all getting used to the heat.

Joan and Audrey enjoying the tap water while washing

[7] *This watch was found by the local police and posted back to my dad's parents in Ceres, South Africa. His dad made a little wooden box for the watch to travel in and posted it to him in London where he received it, 7 months after it was stolen. The wooden box still survives today, the watch however is no longer!*

Joan and Audrey doing washing

Monday, 20th January 1958

Got up early, 4 am to dress and pack up so that we were at Dar es Salaam airport by 6 am to catch the plane for Zanzibar. Managed to get there on time after a bit of a struggle. Flew to Zanzibar in an East African Airways seven-seater plane. Cost us each £3-10-0 each. The flight took 35 minutes each way. It was a clear day and we flew at 5000 feet and could see all the coral reefs. The sea was a glorious blue. On arriving at Zanzibar we took a taxi into town. Very narrow streets, you can almost touch both walls with outstretched hands. Immediately we set foot out of the taxi the curio dealers arrived trying to get us to buy. We couldn't understand them. Did a 2½ hour tour by taxi in the morning. A very interesting drive. Saw cloves, cinnamon and cocoa nuts growing under cultivation. Picked cloves myself. Saw the sultan's two palaces. Very spacious palaces. Saw coconuts drying in the sun. Went over a cocoa nut oil factory. Very interesting but smelly. Mind you we're getting used to the smells out here. I was very hot. What wonderful beaches all around the island. The spear fishing must be excellent, but we didn't have much time to try it. Saw an old Arab slave trading hideout, very grim, built on the beach underground. Had some rest on the beach during the lunch break, we were all tired and hot. Walked along the beach front back towards the central city. Went to the Zanzibar Hotel for afternoon tea – we had had breakfast there as well. The tea was good. Sat in the lounge and wrote letters while waiting for the taxi to take us back to the airport. Flew back to Dar es Salaam in a Dakota of the E.A. Airways. Terrific view from the plane. Camped again at Oyster Beach. Had a swim and then a shower. Supper we were all famished. Wrote letters and then had tea and sat and talked, a real wonderful day. The Zanzibar cathedral is very beautiful.

The 5 heading to Zanzibar

Tuesday, 21st January 1958

Got up late for a change and wrote letters while the rest slept late. Went for a swim then had a shower at the main Carel had found. It was terrific. Went to the police stations to see if they had found Carel's watch. Took some photos at Government House, the Police boys were very smart. Did some shopping, the fellow in the Chemist shop near the Ashri Monument was very helpful and interested in our trip. Had a drink before leaving Dar es Salaam. Sent some photos home by surface mail. I wonder how long they will take. Left Dar just before 1 pm. It was really very hot, the temperature in the Kombi was 98°F. We managed to travel just over 150 miles. Camped down about 10 miles north of Margoro. It was very hot and nobody wanted supper, lots of beer, tea and cool drinks. We had no mosquitoes, what a relief, so we all sat out for quite a while. Then we all climbed into the Kombi to write letters and read. We are really a very happy family; we have settled down very well indeed. Had some fun over tea. The boys take turns to make our bedtime tea and it usually results in some ragging from Audrey and I. Carel is a dear, he does so much without one asking him to do it. So nice to have him around the place. I will really miss him if and when we part company.

Wednesday, 22nd January 1958 (Take Daraprim)

Up early, we didn't have any wild animals worry us, we had expected visitors during the night as we were camped in such a wild country and had found the remains of a lion killed by our site. Saw our first wild pig run along the road and then cross over, big excitement as they are very dangerous. Travelled to Tanga, all we saw was sisal estates. The biggest sisal growing area in the world. Arrived in Tanga just after 3 pm. Looked around for a camping spot, found one on the beachfront. Went to the Tourist Bureau and met a Mr Beer there in charge. He was very interested in our trip and took us to tea at his flat. How we enjoyed that tea. Then he took us for a swim at the Tanga European Swimming Club. A heavenly spot next to the Tanga Yacht Club. There was a raft in the water, we had great fun on it. Went to the Tanga Club for a beer with Mr Beer. A terrific place right on the seafront. Met some other Tanga residents. It was most enjoyable. Supper, talked and then to bed. Everyone was happy.

Thursday, 23rd January 1958

Had a late sleep this morning, it was so enjoyable. Went to see Mr Beer at the Tourist Office just after 9 am. He gave us a typed-out program for today and tomorrow. Took a lot of trouble over it and we appreciated it. Bought food and then left for Pangani, an old fishing village 30 miles south of Tanga. We had breakfast about 10 miles out of Tanga, how we needed it. There were miles of sisal plantations all along the way. Went into the Kigombe Sisal Estate African village where all the houses have paintings on the outside walls. Never seen anything like it before. They are all done by one Africa who is completely self-taught. All scenes depicting their lives. The animal paintings were the best. We took a lot of photos and the Africans didn't seem to mind, all the children followed us around. Travelled on to Mkoma Inn about 28 miles south of Tanga. They were rebuilding the hotel, so I walked down to the beach with Carel. A wonderful stretch of beach. Parked the Kombi amongst the palm trees and had a swim. Millions of small crabs on the beach, water very warm about 90°F. Played around in the water and nearly drowned each other. Arrived in Pangani just after 3 pm. A typical African village with everyone just sitting around. The usual smelly market and in addition a fresh fish market. Fish sold at 1/- not bad. Visited Grundy's workshop which was most interesting. Mr G.L.O. Grundy is a boat building and metalworker. He turned out to be a very interesting fellow who can tell you more than any book can. He advised us not to worry about going to Mombasa, I wonder what we will do. I hope we go as I am expecting post. Drove back to Tanga and went for a swim at the European Swimming Club. It was heavenly camped along the seafront. Sat outside and watched the stars and talked until 11 pm. There was a sea breeze blowing, most enjoyable.

Paintings at the African village

Sisal Estate African Village

Carel and the beach, Tanga

Friday, 24th January 1958

Had another late morning, these quieter mornings make a nice change. Went in to see Mr Beer just after 9 am. He had arranged for us to see over the Amboni Sisal Factory. We said bye to him as Amboni is on the road to Mombasa. What an energetic old chap he is, pity there aren't a few more like him in the public world. Arrived at Amboni just after 10 am. Met Mr Hauser the Swiss master builder at Amboni and he showed us over the factory. It was very interesting. The factory is situated on the banks of a river, very picturesque. Saw the sisal leaves being crushed, washed, dried and packed. All done by Africans who talk all the time they are working. Carel tried to take some cine shots of them, but they objected quite strongly. Walked around the Amboni African village, saw the village artist at work painting on the outside walls of the houses. Very interesting watching him work. The African's around Tanga seem to be very house proud, all the houses are so neat and clean. Went up to the Hauser's house for morning tea. The Hauser built on a hill overlooking the factory. They have a wonderful view of the hills around. The tea was wonderful, Mrs Hauser was very interested in what she called "our long safari". A charming personality. It was so nice going into a home again. Left Amboni just after 12:30 pm. It was hot but there was a pleasant breeze blowing. We had the breeze all the way to Mombasa which made the journey very pleasant. Passed many miles of sisal and coffee plantations. The road was shocking. Crossed the border into Kenya, Carel was the one who had to sign as the car owner. The Kenya roads seemed a little better. Arrived at the south bank Ferry too late to cross. Took a bungalow at Mr Brundy's campground. Had a swim with Carel, showered, had supper, wrote letters by electric light!

Saturday, 25th January 1958

Up early to cross the Likoni Ferry onto the Mombasa Island. Very modern motorboat ferry. Went to the Immigration office, Marius forgot his passport at the camp so we had to wait for him. Received post from home, went for tea, but Audrey wasn't feeling too well. Carel and I walked around Mombasa while the others went back to camp to fetch our bathing costumes. The African market was very interesting, plenty of fruit and bought a good supply. Walked through the Arab shopping centre, they were closed for lunchtime but the buildings were very interesting. Carved doors with at least three locks on each. Bought some native woodwork from the street vendors. There is so much colour in the Mombasa street. Very modern shops and cinemas in the main street. Went out to Nyali for the afternoon. Swam in front of the hotel, a big holiday crowd on the beach, and lots of unattached fellows on the beach. Carel and I walked along the coral reef, there are all kinds of fish and shells in the pools, one could spend hours there. Back to camp for supper and Carel and I walked over the Pontoon Bridge at Nyali. Got dressed and went dancing at the Shelly Beach Hotel. Johan and Marius were not very keen to start with, but they warmed up. Not a big crowd, but it was very pleasant dancing outside. I enjoyed myself dancing with Carel.

Ferry crossing to Mombasa

Sunday, 26th January 1958

Got up late and spent the morning in camp cleaning up and doing washing. The boys serviced the car. Had a fruit lunch, wrote letters. Mr Bundy lent us some goggles so we went goggling. Walked about half a mile out on the coral reef. It was very interesting. Carel and I swam on the reef with the goggles. I have never seen anything like it before. The fish were all colours of the rainbow and we saw millions of them. Saw starfish 16 inches diameter and brilliant colour. Even the seaweed was all colours. Saw coral from pure white to deep reds and purples. It was magnificent. Really enjoyed the afternoon very much. Our last swim in the sea. What a job we had getting back to shore, the tide was coming in and we could see the rocks and pools very clearly. Went back to camp for supper – wrote letters and read, to bed early. A most enjoyable day.

Monday, 27th January 1958

Up very early as we have a lot to do before leaving Mombasa. After a bit of chasing we left the camp just after 8:30 am. Bought provisions and while Audrey, Marius and Johan went to the market Carel and I walked the old harbour. A very smelly walk but a fascinating one, the streets were so narrow that no cars were allowed in. Saw quite a few dhows in the old harbour, watched them loading cargo, the African's chant all the time they are working and it lends an air to the harbour. Took quite a lot of photos, hope they come out. Bought some pure silk at one of the street stores. Left Mombasa at 11:30 am, it was very hot. The boys were very much on edge, couldn't make out what is happening. The road was very wide, dusty and covered in red sand. Arrived at the Voi Hotel just after 3 pm to find we had a flat wheel. The boys nearly had a stand-up fight about who was going to mend it. Thought Audrey and I would have to do it. After about 10 mins talking, they got down to do it. Audrey and I wrote letters. Johan was the one who slipped up, he should have got the spare fixed in Dar es Salaam. Drove on and entered Tsavo National Game Park at the Voi entrance. The petrol pump of the Kombi packed up just after we had entered the park, Johan fixed it. Talk about fun and games. The boy's tempers were flying high by now. Went to the game warden's office and met Peter Jenkins the Game Warden. What a nice fellow he turned out to be. He was very helpful. Took us to see his two pet baby elephants. They were both about 3½ years old and were just about the size of the Kombi. Very tame, loved the oranges we gave them. Travelled on to the Aruba Dam Safari Camp and camped the night there. I had a bilious attack and really felt lousy. As soon as we pitched camp I was as sick as a dog, could have died quite peacefully. Audrey did supper, I didn't have any. Carel made up my bed and I went to sleep early. Surprisingly, but I slept like a log.

Baby elephants

Tuesday, 28th January 1958

Up early to get on the road to see a lot of animals. What a job to get Audrey going. I had washed dresses and filled the flasks before she was 100% conscious. Left Aruba at 7 am. Travelled all along the Voi River. Saw some elephants, eland, springbok, waterbuck, and water hogs. Parked the car at the entrance to Lugards Fall and walked over. It was very hot; the falls ran over some very queer shaped rocks. More like a series of rapids than a fall. From Lugards Falls we motored 39 miles to Mudanda Rock. Along this stretch we saw very little wild life. At Mudanda Rock we climbed into the water house. There we sat for six hours waiting for the elephants to come and drink. We had tea up there overlooking the pool, filled in the time writing letters and reading. Had a very interesting afternoon. While we were there a troupe of baboons arrived to drink. I have never seen such big ones, some were easily 150 lb – 200 lb in weight. Then some water hogs arrived and they played around for long enough. Just after 4 pm the elephants started to arrive, then a giraffe arrived. How clumsy he looked alongside the elephants. By the time we left at 6:10 pm there were 52 big elephants splashing around in the pool. I have never seen so many elephants together at once. They were also some very small baby elephants in the herds. The guide boys were very quick at seeing the elephant in the bush. Peter Jenkins arrived earlier and sat with us for a long time. A real nice chap. Left Mudanda very late with the result that we had to camp down in the dark very near the Savo Station. It's not funny pitching camp and cooking in the dark. Anyway we managed. I was in a real pensive mood so I didn't join in with the usual camp chatter.

Waiting at the water hole

The lookout at the water hole

Wednesday, 29th January 1958 (Take Daraprim)

I got up early but as things turned out it was unnecessary. The boys had to work on the car, a bolt in the generator had worked loose. They spent three hours on the car and managed to fix the trouble. We had another flat tyre which Marius took off and Audrey mended. I sat and wrote some thank you letters for the five of us. Left Tsavo at 11:15 am and reached Mac's Inn at Mtito Andei. What a nice spot – the boys had a drink there. There was a very quaint bar in the corner of the lounge. Entered Tsavo National Park (west) again at the Mtito Andei entrance. Went to see the game warden – David Lovatt-Smills. He had been warned that we were coming and he turned on the charm. He mapped out a route for us and gave us one of his scout boys. From his house to the springs, we saw an assortment of bucks, giraffes and zebras. What a heavenly spot Mzima springs is. The water is crystal clear and from the observation post you can look down at the fish swimming and hippos walking on the riverbed under the water, it was quite weird. From Mzima we took the African scout boy and how quickly he spotted the game. He took us on a circular drive to see if we could find any rhino and how we found rhino. Johan was driving and all of a sudden as we came over a rise the boy shouted "rhino". Well it was too late – there was a mother and her baby right by the side of the road. What happened next was so quick that we didn't have much chance to register properly. She put down her head and charged. I looked up to see about two tons of rhino coming for us. We couldn't avoid her, Johan swung the Kombi off the road but she hit us on the non-drivers side. What a crash, she bust the light completely and buckled the door and front so badly that we can't open the door[8]. Fortunately for us she didn't come back, but made off into the bush. We found out why a few minutes later, there was a lion after her calf. Our lucky day. We beat a hasty retreat to Mzima Springs where we camped amongst the hippos. It was bright moonlight and I wasn't at all happy about the animals[9].

---

[8] *Audrey was sitting in the front passenger seat and lifted her legs to avoid them getting crushed. The scout boy screamed "kwenda, na kwenda" (go! go!), however Johan only just managed to swing sideways. For a crazy moment the car was lifted in the air and then it crashed back down still on all four wheels. They were extremely lucky that the damage did not compromise the Kombi and they could continue travelling.*

[9] *My mum was at the rear of the Kombi cooking, heard a noise, lifted her torch and shone it in the eyes of a hippo a couple meters away. Needless to say she did some rather impressive Olympic winning athletic maneuvers and found safety in the Kombi!*

Rhino hit

The front passenger damage

Tsovo park

George Travel Quartet charged by Rhino

The tempo of experience and high adventure is quickening for the four young people who are travelling up through Africa in their cleverly converted Kombi en route from George to Europe — and beyond. Joan Povall, Audrey Nives and the two Marais brothers were last heard of just before they left Nairobi for Addis Ababa, their next point of contact.

Writing in blazing heat from Mzima Springs in the famous Royal Tsavo National Park,

charged by a rhino, which could well have spelt disaster had Johan Marais not done

the wheel, and so diverted the full direct force of the animal's attack.

WRECKED

As it was the "non-driver's side of the Kombi has been completely wrecked, and the door is so buckled that we can't open it," Joan writes. "The light has also had it."

An African scout was accompanying them through the Reserve, and they had seen all manner of big game at close quarters, when they breasted a rise and suddenly came upon a rhino mother and her calf resting beside the road.

THE CHARGE

Before the party had gathered their wits the rhino charged the Kombi, snorting furiously, and making amazing speed considering its enormous size.

Johan crashed down into low gear and tried to swerve off the road — and so they missed being pierced by the rhino's horn.

The rhino's shoulder caught the side of the car with a resounding crash, throwing it completely off the road. And then, to the party's relief the rhino roared off into the bush with her calf racing behind her.

LION CHASE

The men had just climbed out to inspect the damage done to their vehicle when, to their surprise, a lion leapt out of the bush and gave chase to the rhino!

Nor was that all the excitement for one day. Later, when Joan was cooking the evening meal at the improvised "kitchen" at the back of the Kombi, she heard a noise behind her in the bush. Turning, she shone her torch in its direction—and did the smartest leap into the comparative safety of their home-on-wheels that she had ever done.

AND A HIPPO

A large hippo stood blinking at her in the light of the torch, only 120 feet away!

It says a lot for the girls' nerves that they all ate a good supper there at their camp beside Mzima Springs, and slept soundly — the girls in the Kombi, the men in their low tent.

From Dar es Salaam the party kept to roads that hugged the beautiful coast as far as possible, enjoying bathes in the brilliantly blue sea with its fringe of towering ococonut palms, and making the acquaintance of people in the small towns they visited on their way. Two very full days were spent at Tanga where they evidently saw everything and did everything that there was to see and do.

The kindness they have received all the way has been a wonderful experience, Joan declares.

Although Tanga is about the size of Oudtshoorn, they enjoyed wonderful amenities at the Tanga Club between swims. The Club House is built on the sea-front, with beautiful lawns running down to the water. It has a library, billiard room, table tennis, open air ballroom with a sprung floor, and restaurant.

CORAL REEFS

They also enjoyed many hours on the coral reefs watching the undersea life through goggles and breathing through snorkels — skin diving, in fact. The sea in those parts is full of wonderfully vivid and unusual fish, and the coral ranges in colour from pure white to deep purple, with greens and blues in between.

From Dar es Salaam they flew to Zanzibar in a 7-seater East African Airways plane. The coast looked quite perfect in the early morning, studded with palm-covered islands, and the sea looking like a vast lake.

BY ARABS

They were interested to find the Standard Bank at Zanzibar entirely run by Arabs, and most efficiently, too. As there are only about 360 Europeans on the island, this is hardly surprising.

Hiring a taxi for the morning, they drove all round the island, visiting a large coconut oil factory, and driving through the palace grounds of the Sultan of Zanzibar — the palace is a beautiful pure white mansion set in a theatrically lovely setting.

Mangoes "the size of your woods, Mum," — as Joan describes them to her bowls-enthusiast mother, — pure silk for three or four shillings a yard, wonderful hospitality from Game Reserve wardens, Government officials and private citizens alike, are all discussed in lively style by Joan in her letters home to George.

Nor will any of them ever forget the Kariba Dam, with its mushroom town the size of George that has grown up almost over-night to accommodate the great army of technicians and builders who are making what will be the largest man-made lake in the world — 200 miles wide and 30 miles long!

THE DAM

Because Carel Marais is an engineer it was possible for the party to be shown all over the Kariba construction work, "an experience to make one wonder at man's achievement."

But all that is now behind the wanderers. They are now making their slow way up through Ethiopia to Addis Ababa — where letters will await them, plus some amenities of civilisation.

A newspaper clipping dated 21 February, 1958 reporting the charging rhino incident

Thursday, 30th January 1958

Didn't sleep well at all last night, too many animals walking around. Got up early and travelled back to Mzima Springs to pick up David Lovatt-Smills scout boy. Went to David's office to tell him all about our adventure with the rhino. He was surprised as ours was the first such adventure he had heard of at Tsavo. He was pleased we went to show him the damage[10]. Left David just after 10:30 am for Nairobi. The main road to Nairobi is very wide – 50 ft and they call it a murram road which is what we call gravel in South Africa. Had to fix another flat. Good road but very dusty, by the time we reached Nairobi our hair and clothes were dull red in colour, the dirtiest I have felt on the trip so far. I didn't get out of the car. Carel, Audrey and Marius did our shopping and looked for the S.A. Consulate. We were too late for anything else. Nairobi is a rambling modern city with very wide roads. All down the centre of the main roads there are flower beds. The first time I have seen a "golden-shower" growing flat along the ground. The flowers were really beautiful. I would have liked to go for a swim to clean up a bit but the others couldn't make up their minds, I get a bit tired of the indecision at times. If only the rest would say yes or no sometimes instead of "I don't mind" or "I suppose so". One doesn't really know what they want then. I'm a bit afraid I bulldoze when such an occasion arises, at least we get results then. We couldn't find a camp spot at all. Nairobi hasn't got a camp spot which is really surprising considering its position in Kenya. We rode around for quite a while looking for water and Audrey directed us to a camp spot along the Ngong Hills, very near the Nairobi National Park. We eventually found quite a nice spot in the Langata Quarry. Cooked supper and sat outside for quite a while. It was quite cool, we all had jerseys on for the first time since leaving the Union. I enjoyed the cool breeze very much. Audrey was feeling so hot, she does get tired very quickly, she tries so hard to keep up.

Friday, 31st January 1958

Up early and drove into Nairobi. Went straight to the S.A. High Commissioner to collect mail. I got five letters – it is so nice receiving them all. Went along to see the Ethiopian Consulate to get our visas. What a business to have tourists in Ethiopian. We had to fill in four forms. Had tea in town and then

---

10 *The Kombi completed the rest of the trip in this bashed state with the front passenger door not working. It got repaired in London before being shipped back to South Africa.*

we all split up. Audrey, Johan and Marius took the Kombi and went to look up some friends of Audrey's and Carel and I walked around Nairobi. We had to see the AA and get a permit for the Northern Frontier. I went in to see Lydia Nannucci at the SA Mutual, it was good to see her again, she invited us back to her flat for a bath etc. Carel and I went to the market. What a clean place especially after all the ones we have seen recently. We bought some very nice wood carvings at the market and are going to parcel them up and send them home. I'm so pleased that Carel also wants to do and see as much as possible, the other three don't seem to be very interested in walking around, they say it is too hot, poor things. At 5 pm we met up with Audrey's friends who showed us the way out to their home where we were going to camp. What a long way out, just on 25 miles and a long uphill climb. It was so nice getting into a home again. John and Muriel are very easy people to get on with and really made us feel at home. We had tea with them and then pitched camp while Muriel washed the baby. We had a very nice camp spot overlooking a valley. We were 7542 ft up so it was very chilly indeed, we all had jerseys on. We cooked our own supper, had fresh meat for a change, it was so nice. After supper we went inside and sat talking to Muriel and John. We all had hot baths which were heaven sent. Never thought I would appreciate a hot bath like I did that one. It was heaven just lying in the hot water. After our baths we sat and chattered over a cup of coffee and then we were off to bed. John is a very nice person, got his head screwed on the right way. It was so nice getting into bed after a nice hot bath. I slept like a log even though it was much colder than we had experienced since leaving the Union.

Saturday, 1st February 1958

Got up at 5:30 am because we had to be in Nairobi at 8 am. After a breakfast of egg and bacon, which Muriel cooked at 6 am, we left only to find that we had a flat tyre. So our early morning rising was wasted while the boys fixed it. Got into Nairobi at 8:45 am split company so that we could each do as we wished. I went to the Library to write letters. We all met up at 1 pm and went to the market for fresh veg. Went to Lydia's flat to do the washing in her machine. What luxury, our washing was very dirty. Audrey and I spent all afternoon washing. Carel wrote letters and Johan and Marius went swimming. Had a very nice tea at the flat. Cooked our own supper somewhere out on the Ngong road and then went back to the flat to dress for the bio. Saw "Rock Around the Clock" and really enjoyed the show, as did Audrey and Carel, the other two didn't care for the music which to my mind made the show. After bio we met Lydia and went 10 miles out of Nairobi to the new Castle Hotel to dance. Terrific setting, the dance floor was outside, a circular black marble one which was pure heaven to dance on. Carel and I really went to town and must say I enjoyed the dancing very much. I am afraid the others didn't dance at all, just sat. Carel had to look after Lydia as well. Got back to our camp spot just after 2:45 am. I didn't get to sleep until just after 3 am – slept well.

Sunday, 2nd February 1958

After the late night everyone except me slept late. I got up just after 8 am and sat outside in my pyjamas writing letters etc. After an hour or so Carel joined me. We gave the rest breakfast in bed, they did not get up until 10:30 am. Went to Lydia's flat, sat talking there until it was time to leave for the African Tribal dancing. Audrey and Johan didn't come with us, they took the Kombi and went to see the escarpment. Had to queue up to get into the tribal dancing, for nearly an hour we battled. What fun, it was an education watching the crowd and the policemen. The dancing was excellent. Very different to our SA native dances, the rhythm was also different. The dress was also more primitive and most colourful. I enjoyed it very much, took a lot of photos, saw my first African Band. Lydia took us for a drive around Nairobi, a spreading beautiful city. Supper at the flat and then camped at Langata Quarry.

Tribal dancing show in Kenya

Monday, 3rd February 1958

Had to get up early, but I'm getting tired of chasing the three late ones. It's not fair as they know as well as I do that to get away to a good start we must all get up early. We had a lot of bits and pieces to do in Nairobi, sat and wrote letters to catch the airmail and did up and posted a parcel of wood carvings home. Met an American couple in the street that was very interested in our trip. They were heading for South Africa so Audrey and I gave them our home addresses, I hope they look the folks up. Audrey and I went out to lunch with an old friend of hers, Mr George Vamos, a Hungarian Architect. He took us to the Equator Inn. Started with a sherry which we drank sitting on stools at the bar counter, I like the idea of women being allowed in the bar! The bars up here are most beautifully decorated. We had lunch amidst a most delightful setting. The dining room was well appointed and the service excellent. Audrey and I had roast duck with all the trimmings and George had trout. Then we had cold pudding mixture which was delicious, even had fresh cherries. Finished off with coffee. The best meal we have had since leaving home. I felt so sleepy afterwards not being used to a big mid-day meal. Went to say cheerio to Lydia and then left Nairobi just after 2:30 pm. We were on our way to see George and Dawn Parsons at Fort Hall. Got there to find that he had been transferred to Embu a further 25 miles on. Got to Embu just at 6 pm, and finally tracked them down, unpacking boxes at their new home. Dawn was very surprised to see me and very thrilled. We all went over to the Izak Walton Hotel for a drink, sat talking until just at 8:30 pm. Dawn and George let us use the empty house for the night. Cooked our supper on the lawn and ate it there. They have a wonderful view from their lawn, there was a very bright moon shinning. Had cold baths and did some washing and then settled down to letter writing and reading. Got to bed after 12 pm, much to all our surprise, we didn't realise it was so late.

Dawn's House, Embu

Tuesday, 4th February 1958

Had a good night's sleep. I slept in the Kombi on my own, the rest slept in the empty house. Said good-bye to George and Dawn and left for Isiolo. Travelled through country very like the old road between George and Knysna. It was lovely, climbed up one side of the mountain and down the other side. Mt Kenya was on our left all day, towards mid-day it became overcast and we didn't see the summit again. Had morning tea at a waterfall. It was lovely clear water and so cool. Our traveller friend of the night before had tea with us[11]. The area

[11] *Somewhere along the way a mouse had decided to take up residence in the Kombi. Unfortunately he made a bit of a nuisance of himself and further along the journey a mousetrap was bought. I like to think it was unsuccessful in killing the mouse.*

we travelled through was very heavily populated with Africans, in fact over populated in places. Mostly Kikuyu – a very tall fine-looking race. Their women seemed to be beasts of burden. They did all the work it seems, even carrying heavy loads slung down their backs from a leather strip over their foreheads. The older ones have quite a grove on their foreheads from always carrying such heavy loads. They're mostly farmers. We passed quite a few mission stations, really big settlements. Arrived at Isiolo just after 4 pm, and had to wait to see the D.C. to get a permit to travel though the Northern Frontier area. Watched the African guard change, very smart boys dressed in khaki shorts, white bush jackets and red turbans. Got our permit and set forth in a convoy with two trucks for Wajir. We soon managed to lose the trucks. Beautiful country, mountainous with plains in between. Saw plenty of giraffes, zebras, Thompson gazelle (just like our springbok only bigger), dik dik, vultures and our first herd of camels. Also passed a police patrol unit, five African police boys on camels. We really feel as if we are far from home now. Saw quite a few ostriches – something I didn't quite expect to see outside the Dol area. Camped about 60 miles from Isiolo, bright moonlight and very hot. We'll have to go back on salt tabs again!!!

Border crossing

Wednesday, 5th February 1958 (Take Daraprim)

Got up early to get a good start before the heat started. The countryside is getting more and more desert-like. Saw quite a bit of game, especially giraffes. They're very dark brown in colour up here. I spent all morning typing letters as we travelled along, a good day's work. This is a very lonely stretch without water or petrol. Got very hot during the day, we were all sweating quite freely. The road was very sandy and we got stuck because we moved over to pass another car. Had to get out and push, it was easy, really. Arrived at Wajir just before 3 pm. What a strange place, all set up in the middle of a desert built on top of a limestone area, it is very hot. Plenty of very big anthills all over the place. Carel went to see the D.C. and left us outside with just about all the children in the place climbing all over the Kombi, what fun. The D.C. allowed us the use of the

Royal Wajir Yacht Club house for the night. Gordon Cairns, the D.O., showed us around and gave us a beer, nice chap. Audrey, Carel and I went to buy provisions, all the population seemed to go with us. My but they are a curious lot and also so sticky. Had a bath and hair wash which was terrific. The water was brackish but we didn't mind. Cooked supper early as we had been invited by the D.C. to join them at their club for the evening. Spent the evening on the roof, drank orange squash the whole night, it was very cool up there and the moon was full. Met two police officers, the doctor and also a couple travelling south. I spent quite a long while chatting to a visiting police sergeant. He was most interesting. The D.C., Mr Mathews, was very intriguing, the strong silent type who commands attention whenever he is present. I would have liked to spend more time in his company, he caught my imagination, guessing. The boys and Audrey slept on the roof and I had the Kombi to myself. The moonlight was too bright to sleep outside for my liking.

NFD Wajir

Wajir House, Audrey on the roof

Wajir

Thursday, 6th February 1958

Had a very nice awakening from the Muslim priest chanting from the mosque roof. What a racket and then before the sun rose!! Went to say cheerio to everyone and joined our convoy of escort transport trucks just after 8 am. It was very hot and I was feeling lousy, had lost my sense of balance due mainly to sweating and the intense heat. Never saw the trucks again after we left Wajir. I slept most of the way and sweated like a pig. It was terribly hot. Carel was concerned that I had started a dose of malaria but I was sure that I hadn't. The road was bad, a sandy track with a very high middle mannetjie. It slowed us a lot. Saw a lot of buck and in places clouds of locusts rose up in front of the Kombi. At times the country was very barren with hundreds of ant hills scattered all over the place. Some were easily twice the size of the Kombi. Saw a lot of nomad shepherds with their goats and camels. Saw quite a few camel caravans, would like to have taken some photos but they are too shy, they leave the road long before you reach them. Had tea at Buma Spring, a natural well of brack water where the camels will drink as much as 44 gals at one time. No wonder they can go without water for so long. The approach to Moyale was so steep that the four of us had to get out and walk up the hill. Moyale is just a police post on the border. European population of 4! They have about 200 Ashri police boys stationed here, very smart boys. Met the police Sgt in charge – Hammond. He was very nice to us and allowed us to camp very near his house. After we had our supper, he invited us to have a drink with him. He allowed Audrey and I to use his bathroom, had a lovely hot bath and hair wash. One feels quite human again. Sat and chattered to Sgt Hammond until 11:30 pm. He was most interesting. Put quite a show on for us; savouries, beer for the chaps and ice lime juice for Audrey and I, we did appreciate it. Saw a lot of hyenas around our camp spot when we went to bed so we had to pack all our food etc in the Kombi.

Friday, 7th February 1958

Got up early to get through the customs and immigrations quickly. Millions of locusts swarmed overhead as we approached Moyale, it made the sky quite black. Had to wait for a signal to come through regarding the Customs and our deposit on the roof carrier of the Kombi. Waited in the police station and wrote letters and read. The others bought the petrol and food for our long lonely trip to Addis Ababa. Waited until nearly 1 pm and then gave up and left without our deposit. Crossed into Ethiopia just after 1 pm, what a crew. They couldn't understand us and we couldn't understand them. After quite a battle we satisfied them and they let us continue along the Great Northern Road. Why they call it great I don't know, it is in a terrible state of repair. We have groused about the Tanganyika roads, but these are far worse. We travelled all day without meeting another car. Took us six hours to transverse the 64 miles from Moyale to Mega, we had to get out and push the Kombi a few times. Saw a lot of very big anthills. Climbed down a cattle well, quite an education. The wells are hand dug and go down about 80 feet. The herdsmen climb down and pass goats bladders full of water up to the top where they are emptied into a trough where the animals drink. The smell was not so good, wouldn't like to drink the water myself. The countryside looked very barren yet the cattle and camels looked extremely well fed. The natives in Ethiopia are not a proud race, the men aren't so bad but the women are really ugly. They are also a very dirty crowd. Travelled until it was dark to try to reach the British Consulate's house outside Mega. Luck was against us, the Kombi would not pull up the hills approaching Mega so we had to get out and walk which made us late. Then it started to rain, the poor Kombi battled up to Mega. What a dump, the police couldn't understand English so we battled on towards the Consulate's house. Too late to knock him up so we camped in the grounds of the Ethiopian police. All the neighbourhood turned out to watch us pitch camp. It rained hard while we had supper. I had a headache.

Getting the Kombi up the hill

Saturday, 8th February 1958

How it rained during the night. Thought we were going to be washed away. After breakfast we drove up to the English Consulate's house to find that he had gone to Addis. The boy there told us that the rains had started and that we should be careful. And how the rains had started. Took us four hours to do the first 20 miles out of Mega. We pushed the Kombi for the first time, even had to use the block and tackle. It was real hard work with the Kombi down to her axle in the mud. In one place we battled for ¾ hour and then as our luck would have it, a Land Rover driven by an African pitched up. They towed us out. After that the road seemed to become less muddy. We tried our hand at shooting partridges and guinea fowl, after dozens of shots, Johan bagged one. He and Audrey cleaned it, should make a good supper. Camped down the night outside Yabelo. Had our first wood fire, it was so nice sitting outside, wrote this up, read and talked. Had an argument with Carel about the Voortrekker monument.

Helping Hand

Muddy tracks

Muddy roads

Stuck

Sunday, 9th February 1958

Up early, our food is running short, no more bread, will have to make it up with tinned beans, rice and potatoes. Hope the boys' won't mind. Travelled through Siroppa, Aghremariam, San Malo, all small native villages. How they stared at us, I'm sure many of them haven't seen white people before. The country is very mountainous but being cloudy we couldn't see very much, it must look terrific in the sunlight. The roads are very rocky and it is slow going, we are in first gear most of the time again. Passed through quite a few native villages, they all seem very poor and also extremely dirty. Again the women seem to do all the work and are very deformed. Some of them are a real eye sore. Camped down that night just outside Aghremariam. The natives sang all night, we were a bit worried that they might worry us but they didn't. Ate the guinea fowl for supper. It was delicious, just like chicken.

Curious visitors in Ethiopia

Spectacular views

Driving through villages

Monday, 10th February 1958

Broke camp early to try and avoid the flies. There are millions of them and they are very trying. It had rained during the night with the result that the roads were very muddy and wet, what a battle we had to keep the Kombi going. Our first 18 miles took us five hours, pure determination and brute force. What hard work, how we sweated. We used the spade, brought in rocks and used the block and tackle largely as we pulled and pushed our way up all the hills, on the slippery hills we had to dig footholds in order to push. I have never battled so hard and never seen a car struggle so much. Fortunately for us the countryside was fairly well populated so we got quite a bit of help from the locals. In fact without their help we would not have got up some of the hills. At times the Kombi was axled deep in mud. We even had to jack her up twice. Once she slid on a wooden bridge and got the back right hand wheel jammed between two logs. What fun, but the boys were marvellous through it all. With much patience they set to every time with a determination that really surprised me. The local natives, materializing from nowhere, would sit alongside the road and watch and then when they were convinced that we couldn't manage they would rally round and help, each one shouting louder than his neighbour. They could not understand us and we could not understand them. As it grew hotter the road improved slightly and we did the last 19 miles to Dilla in two hours. We had to buy food and petrol at Dilla but had a job trying to change money as there is no bank at Dilla. Managed to buy some bread for the first time since leaving Nairobi a week ago. We made real pigs of ourselves with bread, butter and jam. I am sure we missed the bread, each one of us. Don't think I have ever enjoyed bread and butter so much. After supper we all went to bed very tired indeed. Today proved that we can all work together very well especially for our mutual welfare. Audrey and I have given up driving – I think the boys are really relieved, they are definitely the better drivers on the rough roads.

Road Struggles

Great Northern Road

Road conditions

Building roads

Villagers help

A petrol station in Ethiopia

Tuesday, 11th February 1958

We were camped at Lake Awassa (???) for the day.

We had camped down about 20 miles north of Wendo, had been looking for a freshwater lake to camp alongside but it got dark before we got there. Anyway Carel got up early and made tea, then the other two got up and the boys gave Audrey and I breakfast in bed. It was so nice, only the second time I have had breakfast or tea in bed since we left Pretoria. Travelled about 20 miles on good gravel roads and found the lake. Camped down just after 11 am. Had a swim in the lake and did some washing. It was nice to be clean again after all the dirt and mud yesterday. The local natives all gathered around and try as we might, we couldn't get rid of them, they talk all the time. We must be like the zoo to them. It was a beautiful day and our washing dried very quickly. Carel and I went for a walk to explore the countryside, walked quite a way along the road and then cut down to the lake. It was very hot and the flies were a big nuisance. We found some big flat rocks on the edge of the lake and lay there for a long time. Talked about what we were going to do when we reached London. It was nice being lazy after the hard work of yesterday. I must admit that I really enjoy Carel's company – he is the ideal travelling companion. Johan is too set in his ways and Marius is inclined to get on my nerves, he is so quiet and thinks he always knows best. If I could have picked my travelling companion I would have left the two of them in S.A. But it is amazing our combination seems to work even though we are all so different. Mind you if it wasn't for Carel I don't think I would be enjoying the trip. After our walk Carel serviced the Kombi and I wrote letters, Audrey painted and Johan and Marius read. I cooked supper and then we packed up and went to bed. We chattered quite a while about nothing in particular. Johan and Marius never seem to have anything to say for themselves.

Wednesday, 12th February 1958 (Take Daraprim)

Got up early to try and miss the flies. Got away just after 8 am. The lake looked terrific so early in the morning. What a difference a good road makes, it was gravel but well-kept and we managed to do the 170 miles to Addis in seven hours. The country near Addis flattens out quite a bit, rolling plains with hills in the distance. It was very hot and dusty and we were all inclined to be very sleepy. Audrey and I did some driving for the first time since leaving Embu nearly a week ago. The poverty of the inhabitants is really appalling. I expected to see better houses etc. the nearer we approached Addis, but was disappointed. They seem to live in the dirt and squalor even in Addis, it distresses me terribly. No wonder that Ethiopia is such a poor country. We stopped at Shashamane for food and petrol, managed to get fresh bread and meat which will be a most welcome change. Addis Ababa seems to be built on a hill and is very dirty or perhaps I should say the people are very dirty. We fetched the post, one letter from John[12] and one for Carel. That letter from John was a real lifesaver for me, bless him. It was too late for the bank so we drove around Addis for an hour or so. Passed the Imperial Palace, Haille Selaisse's home, what a place with a terrific wall all the way round and the guards at the gate. Somehow the grandeur didn't fit in with the poverty of the surrounding houses. But the emperor is doing his best with the poor material he has, the Africans are not a very intelligent lot. Saw quite a few big schools and colleges. The foreign embassies are also grand places. Camped down near the army rifle range, washed my hair, it was cold.

---

[12] *John was courting Joan at the time of her starting the trip.*

Thursday, 13th February 1958

Got up late, Audrey and I wrote letters in bed. Breakfast and then into Addis to see the Egyptian Consulate. Audrey and Carel went into see him, her visa was refused[13]. Somehow I knew she would not get it. So we set off to visit all the travel agents in Addis to see what they had to offer in the way of bypassing Egypt. We tried to discuss the question of splitting up but didn't get very far for the simple reason that only Carel and I gave our views, Audrey seems afraid to state her view. After all she should be the one to talk the most, she is the only one without an Egyptian visa. After a short tour of the travel agents we decided to leave the decision until we get to Asmara. Hope we can please everyone and not have a fight about the issue. Went and looked around the market, very interesting saw all the workmen at their jobs, really fascinating watching them apply their skill. Carel took us to lunch at an Italian restaurant, it was terrific. Served in the real continental style. We couldn't read the menu which was in Italian so the proprietor came and helped us choose our meal. What fun, we didn't know what to expect when it arrived. Had a type of spaghetti, fried chicken and salads and Italian black grapes. Don't know when I last enjoyed a meal so much. All the time we were eating they played Italian music which made it so much nicer. The restaurant had no colour ban as everywhere else in East Africa, it was a bit strange eating in a café with Africans but they were all the same social standing so it didn't matter. Did some shopping and then left Addis for Asmara. Travelled about 30 miles and camped in an old quarry, it was very cold.

Friday, 14th February 1958

Carel's birthday.

So we celebrated the 2nd birthday on the tour, Carel's. I got up early and gave him early morning coffee in bed, was only just in time as he was just about to get up. The rest had forgotten his birthday, I had to remind them. The country is a terrific wheat farming country which is not really exploited enough. Apples would also grow well there. The natives do farm wheat but only on a very small scale. It was very cold; we all had jerseys, long trousers, shoes and socks on. It was so cosy in the Kombi. Travelled over the Mussolini Pass which is about 20

---

13 *Audrey was travelling on a British passport. Following the Suez Crisis of July 1956, tensions between Britain and Egypt remained high and as a result Audrey had been refused entry to Egypt.*

miles up and 2 miles down. A very good road built by the Italians. Unfortunately we ran into heavy mist half way up the pass so we didn't see very much and missed seeing views of the Rift Valley. Passed a lot of 10-ton transport trucks. We celebrated Carel's birthday by eating the other half of the Christmas cake. It was so nice having hot tea and fruitcake all up in the mist. Passed through four tunnels, one about ½ mile long and very dark inside. The Kombi travelled very well up the steep climbs especially as she is so heavily loaded. Passed a lot of wandering tribesmen with quite big herds of goats and cattle. Travelled as far as Dessie in the mist, had to sleep there under police protection because of armed bandits in the mountains. We couldn't pitch the tent as we were parked in the street outside the police station. Audrey and I were fed up with the boys as they had left camping until it was dark and we had to cook in the mist and dark and it is not funny. They had been arguing as to where we could camp that is why I was fed up. Marius slept on the front seat of the Kombi and the four of us packed like sardines on the back seat.

Views

Saturday, 15th February 1958

Thel & Rod's wedding day.

Woke up to the sound of the police bugle. I was surprised that I managed to sleep so crowded in the Kombi. Marius drove us out of Dessie where we dressed, repacked and cooked breakfast. Thought of Thel and Rod a lot and how the wedding was going. Wondered how mum was feeling, hope not too lonely. I prayed hard that everything would be alright. We travelled through beautiful country, with a very long mountain pass over the escarpment about 80 miles up. Very steep roads winding backwards and forwards across the mountains. The Italians built the passes and they certainly know their engineering stuff. We stopped quite often to take photos. Unfortunately the mist caught up with us again, not really surprising as we climbed from 4,000 ft to 10,000 ft in the matter of about 20 miles. It was very cold up on top. Travelled along the top of the mountain for about 50 miles. The natives' farm high up in the mountains, very small plots but it makes for picturesque scenery. They also keep a lot of goats and cows. Camped early very near a village for safety sake. It was cold, misty and rainy. Listened to the wireless, wrote letters and went to bed, still a bit worried about camping out in the open. I was feeling very homesick and wanted to be with John.

Audrey and the twisting passes

Sunday, 16th February 1958

Up early, for a change Audrey did the flasks and made breakfast. Travelled over the Amba Alan Pass (9800 ft). It was magnificent. We climbed 4000 ft in 10 miles. The pass wound in and out and around the mountains. We had a wonderful view and took a lot of photos. Over the pass on the plateau we stuck heavy mist again and it was very cold. Down in the plain again the vegetation dried out almost to semi-desert very like the Karoo. The mountains were very like Tinus de Jongh's paintings. Took me back home to the Oudstroom district. Johan was in a very blue mood. He is inclined to be almost morose. I'm glad I won't have to spend too much time in his company. I find him very unbending. Camped down just outside Adigrat, it was cold but at least dry.

Audrey photographing the pass switch backs

Passes driven

Monday, 17th February 1958

Up early and it was cold, put my clothes on over my pyjamas. Travelled through barren rugged country. Did plenty of climbing, how the Italians like to make their roads and passes go in and out. The Kombi's accelerator cable broke which Johan and Marius fixed. Passed plenty of old Italian farm houses, they looked so eerie. Passed through the town of Decamere, an old industrial town built up by the Italian's before World War II. Just about every building and house was deserted except for a few native huts built in the gardens of the houses. Some were really beautiful buildings. A catholic church almost the same size as St Mary's Cathedral in George stood out in the centre of the town just like a challenge to all those who had forced the inhabitants out of Decamere. Decamere must have been a big thriving town in its day. Arrived in Asmara just after 3 pm. Collected post and then went to look for travel agents with the view of getting Audrey and I a boat booking or air booking to Europe. They were all closed, business hours being mornings only. Drove around the town looking for a camp spot. Asmara seems a very nice place, very Italian with plenty of Italian shops and people walking around, so nice to see so many Europeans for a change. The streets are nice and wide with flower islands running down the centre of the streets. Went out along the road to Massawa and found a very nice camp spot in a forest reserve. Before long a forestry officer pitched up and asked us what we were doing!! After a long conversation through the medium of a young African schoolboy he decided that we could stay the night. Seems as only the school children talk English. Italian is spoken by everyone, strange hearing the natives talking Italian. We had our first fry of the tour. Managed to get some steak which I fried. We all enjoyed the change, previously we have stewed the fresh meat. We all had a wash down in the tent and took out clean clothes for tramping around Asmara tomorrow.

Asmara Ethiopia

Ethiopian landscape

Tuesday, 18th February 1958

Up early and into Asmara. The Kombi had to go into the garage to have the oil checked. Carel stayed with the Kombi and the rest of us walked from one shipping line to another and then we tried all the airlines. Audrey and I went to the British Consulate for advice on where to stay, either in Khartoum or Athens. The company has decided that Audrey should fly from Khartoum to Athens alone and I travel with the boys through Egypt and then we pick up Audrey in Athens. Johan has decided to go home and is going to fly back to Johannesburg from Khartoum[14]. I am pleased that he has decided to go home because I'm sure he hasn't been enjoying the tour so far, he's just not the adventurous type. Audrey and I went to the Italian Consulate to check up on our visas. We all met up at the Sudanese Consulate where we had a long session with the Vice-Consulate. They are full of nonsense and want a £300 bank guarantee from Carel before they will allow us to motor through Sudan. We also had to get the permission of the Minister of the Interior before we could motor through Sudan and had to telegram him which cost us £2-3-0. Then we still had to wait for his reply. What a business. To cheer ourselves up we went to an Italian restaurant for lunch. It was terrific. I had spaghetti, tomatoes, boiled shrimp and mayonnaise. The first time I have had shrimps and I really like them. We all enjoyed the meal. It is the first time I have seen salad served with a meal like bread and butter, the celery was delicious. In the afternoon we shopped and got our exit permits. Funny to have to pay to leave a country, cost us each 5/6. As tomorrow is an Ethiopian public holiday, public holiday of Independence, we decided to travel the 90 miles down to Massawa and have a look at the port on the Red Sea. Travelled 16 miles down towards Massawa all down a very steep mountain pass, very beautiful scenery.

Wednesday, 19th February 1958 (Take Daraprim)

Wake up early after a very good night's sleep. The scenery around us was lovely. We had camped in the dark last night so we didn't appreciate it. We were camped near a mountain village and as we looked up we could see five curves in the pass. After a lazy breakfast we continued on our way to Massawa. Travelled

---

[14] *Johan was heart sore for a girl he met in Sasolburg. They were corresponding during the trip and the last letter he received from her caused a change of heart for him and so he decided to return back to South Africa. It had a happy ending as this was the person he ended up marrying.*

about 53 miles down through the mountains winding in and out. The road was good but we couldn't get up to speed because of the winding roads. While I was driving, we had a burst tyre. Not so bad, really as I wasn't going very fast, the first burst I have had while driving. Near the coast the land is very barren. The people are terribly poor, one wonders what they live on. Arrived in Massawa just at lunchtime. The approach is lined with little wooden houses all very dirty looking. Drove around having a look at the place, it was a public holiday so all the business places were shut, plenty of flags out. There wasn't much to see, the town is Arabic in one section and Italian in the other, but the whole lot is desolate. Another town built up by the Italians and then let go, plenty of derelict houses, some quite big. We looked for a swimming beach but couldn't find one so we parked on the beachfront. It was very hot, Audrey and I wrote letters, Marius and Johan read and Carel worked on the car. We had tea and sandwiches, made ourselves, and then we set off for Asmara again. It was much pleasanter going back than the trip down, we could see more as there wasn't so much mist about. The pass was beautiful in the late afternoon sun. Camped down again at our last night's camp spot, some camels had wandered in. Audrey and I did some washing, the boys fixed the tyre. Had supper early and then wrote letters. Carel bought me the chocolate I had been wanting for days, it was very nice indeed.

Thursday, 20th February 1958

Got up at 5:30 am as we had to be in Asmara at 9 am to see the bank manager about our guarantee for the Sudanese Govt just to allow us to motor through Sudan. Carel, Marius and I spent 2½ hours with the Bank, Audrey and Johan fixed up their respective air bookings. Johan to fly to Johannesburg on the 25th and Audrey to fly to Athens on the 25th. The Ethiopian State banks were very nice to us. We had to sign £310 worth of travellers cheques and leave them with the bank. They will airmail them on to Athens once the guarantee is cancelled on the 8th March. We were dealt with by an Ethiopian (native) and he couldn't have been more polite, knew his job too. The manager was German and his secretary Italian, very polite as well. From the bank we went back to the Sudanese Consulate only to be told that we would have to wait until 4:30 pm for our visa. We were fed up about this because our Ethiopian visa terminates on the 22nd and it's going to mean a battle against time to get to Kassala before the visa runs out. Drove out of Asmara for our lunch, tea and sandwiches. It was very hot. Back again after lunch to finish off our shopping. Audrey and I went hunting while the boys waited for the visas. Bought the most delicious ice cream I have tasted for a long time. Was quite expensive, 1/6d a small cup, but it was worth it. Left Asmara just after 5 pm and travelled about 35 miles, along the way the retread tyre blew out[15]. Parked on a dry riverbed to have our first braaivleis of the tour. It was a perfect evening and we had chops, potatoes boiled in their jackets and onions done in the fire. I really enjoyed it. Packed up and travelled on until we reached Keren, camped the night near the bowling green. We were all sleepy, had tea and went to bed. Missed the usual hangers on as it was dark, thank goodness.

Friday, 21st February 1958 (Rod's Birthday)

Up early again, rushed breakfast as we are on a race against time to reach the border before tomorrow when our Ethiopian visas terminates. Had fried eggs for breakfast and really enjoyed them. It was very hot, 100°F in the sun, travelled through a very barren country, semi-desert area. Saw quite a few big camel caravans. The villages we passed through were extremely dirty. One can't seem to get away from the dirt and smells here in Ethiopia. I still haven't seen a lavatory here, everyone just uses the street and the smell is terrible. Passed some oasis where we saw camel caravans parked. There was much shouting from all the drivers, couldn't make out whether they were bargaining or just talking to each other. Arrived at the Ethiopian customs at 12:45 to be told that the office only opens again at 4 pm. So we just had to sit around. The boys went for a drink while Audrey and I wrote letters. I washed my hair at a tap next to the customs office while Audrey made a paw paw salad which we ate with some bread and butter. After going through customs we travelled about 15 miles into the Sudan and camped amongst some very curious rock out crops. Great big solid pieces of rock rising out of the flat plain, volcanic origin. I had a headache so Audrey did supper. It was very hot until the sun set. The boys changed the tyres around. After supper we lay outside on the canvas. It was a perfect night and after the heat of the day the cool breeze was most welcome. I think we were all pleased to be out of Ethiopia as they are a real dense lot and everything was very expensive. The most expensive country for food and petrol so far. Slept with the tent flaps up, it was very nice and cool with a continuous breeze. The moon was perfect.

---

15 *This retread tyre was donated by a local business man in Joan's home town of George I think he got his money's worth as the prototype lasted quite a distance despite vigorously testing!*

Kassala scene

Sudan landscape

Saturday, 22nd February 1958

Up early and travelled the odd 10 miles or so into Kassala. At the Customs and Immigration Office we met up with the Customs Officer whom Carel had met before. He was very nice to us and invited us all into his office for tea, a kind of black sweet mint tea, cold. It was strong to taste yet very refreshing. After we had finished with Customs he took some photos of us. The Sudanese are much more educated than the Ethiopians and much more polite. Joseph told us what to do and where to go to see the sights of Kassala. We walked about the market, some old fellow attached himself to us as a guide, a real rogue, but we had some fun at his expense. Bought meat and vegetables and then drove out of town to wait for late afternoon before setting out across the desert for Khartoum. Stopped at an old water well. Carel and I took some photos of the camels and their riders. We slept a bit and ate a watermelon. Set off for Khartoum along a dusty sandy track just after 3:30 pm. It was very hot, 110°F in the Kombi. Travelled until 9 pm when we stopped for supper, had another braaivleis, meat was a bit tough. The sunset was perfect, lit the desert a rich pinkish red. Travelled on again taking turns to sleep in the back. It is certainly better travelling at night in the desert, it is quite bearable as far as the temp goes.

The 5, border crossing

Kassala, Sudan

Sunday, 23rd February 1958

Just at 1 am, we came across a broken-down truck, broken coil. We couldn't help them so we took one of the men in to Khartoum with us for help. He turned out to be a Sudanese Gov telegraph operator from Port Sudan on his way to Khartoum on holiday. He spoke a little English so we managed a bit of conversation with him. Watched the sun rise over the desert, like a red-hot ball coming up over the red sand. Arrived in Khartoum just before 6 am. Found a camp spot along the river Nile where we cleaned up and had breakfast. Audrey and Johan confirmed their air bookings and then we parked for the night along the Nile. Did some washing then Carel and I drove around looking for somewhere to buy tyres. It was very hot. I was surprised at how big and clean Khartoum is. Seems a very nice place. The Nile is very wide.

Monday, 24th February 1958

Up early, I did breakfast while Audrey packed. Wrote some letters. Saw a Nile steamer pass by, it looked so peaceful with its paddle going around. I'm looking forward to the trip on the steamer from Wadi Halfa to Shellal. It soon became very hot. Went into town to buy provisions etc. Audrey and I found a very nice super market that seemed to sell everything. It was so nice being able to pick and choose our food for a change, they had a marvellous selection. Poor old Audrey was feeling a bit out of things knowing that she wouldn't be eating the food with us. I am very sad that she won't be with us, but what else could we do? When we met up again we all had tea etc at the supermarket. I lost my dark glasses and was most upset, but Audrey found them for me on the super market's fridge. Carel was very harassed as he couldn't find anywhere to buy tyres. It was hot so we decided to go out of town and cook our big meal and thus save Audrey and Johan the expense of a main meal. Had our last meal, all five of us together. Audrey and Johan changed and really looked smart alongside the three of us, Carel, Marius and self. Went back into town to finish off our bits and pieces, finally got tyres and extra petrol. Managed to get some very nice fruit at the market. Carel is a real master hand at bargaining with the natives. Think we'll have to delegate him to this job for the rest of the tour. We finished at 6:10 pm and after one last coca cola together, we took Audrey and Johan to the Grand Hotel. Said cheerio. I'm sorry that Johan has decided to go home, he would have benefitted much more from a couple of months work in Europe, it would have knocked off all the rough edges. I was sad to part company with Audrey, even for two weeks. I'm on my own with Carel and Marius now. Had a bit of battle trying to find the way out of Khartoum. After some help from a native we finally got under way. The road was not too clear in the dark. Followed the North Star quite a bit, kept on losing ourselves in small villages.

Tuesday, 25th February 1958

Travelled on until 1:10 am when the clutch cable snapped. Pushed the car off the road and settled down to sleep until dawn. I slept in the Kombi and Carel and Marius outside next to it. Woke just as it was getting light, dressed and made tea. Carel and Marius set to and started putting in a new clutch cable. I made breakfast, fried bread and eggs. It was quite chilly, a big contrast to the day temp. I washed up and filled the flasks and wrote this up. Carel and Marius are struggling to get the cable in. It is beginning to get hot and the wind is blowing, very unpleasant. There is nothing to see for miles around except desert sand and stone, what a country!! Got going again at 10:45 am after wasting five hours travelling time, but the cable was fitted and the car goes again. It is wonderful having the boys around especially as they know all there is to know about the Kombi. After travelling about two hours we struck very soft sand and then our troubles really started. Anyway we managed to keep going and reached Atbara just at sunset. A very big town only a little smaller than Khartoum. It is situated where the Atbara River joins the Nile, very green. Saw a beautiful sunset as we entered the town. Very big industrial centre with a massive cement factory which has a cable car line running direct to the Nile. A very modern idea in the midst of all the primitiveness. Stopped for petrol and water at a Shell garage and soon collected the usual crowd. Couldn't find our way out of Atbara, then some fellow on a bicycle showed us the way out. I have never seen anyone ride a bicycle so fast. How we laughed. Travelled on until we got too stuck to do anything about it (2:18 am). By this time we were also too tired. I slept in the Kombi which was at a crazy angle and the boys slept outside next to the car. What a day.

Sandy Tracks

Car care

Wednesday, 26th February 1958 (Take Daraprim)

Got up again as soon as dawn broke and started to get the Kombi out of the sand. How we battled, after about ¾ hour digging, pushing and sweating we got her moving only to get stuck a little further on. There does not appear to be a road just millions of tracks across the desert. At about 11 am while we were struggling to get out of a sand drift a lorry rolled up. Gosh! Were we pleased to see him. He pulled us out and from then on we travelled together. We would dig and push him out and they did likewise for us. Just after 2 pm we were joined by two buses. So we formed a small convoy and travelled together helping each as we got stuck. The poor Kombi took a real battering. Carel did most of the driving and was as careful as possible, but she kept on getting hit underneath. We had let the tyre down to 10 lbs in front and 15 lbs at the back, this helped a lot in the sand, but on the rock outcrops she continually hit down. I am sure that without the help of the trucks we wouldn't have got through so quickly. We had been travelling non-stop since Khartoum and even then we were just running short of three hours time. By late afternoon we were all very tired and dirty, none of us had washed since Khartoum. I have never felt so dirty before. The clutch started slipping just after 4 pm and then Carel really started to worry. We still had 250 miles to travel before catching the Steamer at Wadi Halfa and only 16 hours to do it in. Reached Abu Hamad just before sunset very tired and dirty, but determined to drive right through the night. After reporting to the police we were invited to have tea with the Met Officer and his wife (Africans). How we enjoyed the tea. Bought petrol and filled up with water, set off just after 8 pm with a police truck to show us the way out. Had a supper of sandwiches and then got going.

Help at hand

Desert convoy

Convoy companions

Letting the tyres down

Thursday, 27th February 1958

This stretch from Abu Hamad to Wadi Halfa is pure desert and our only quibble is the railway lines which we followed. Without it I'm sure we would have lost our way completely. We had used the stars the previous two nights but with the railway line and telephone line it wasn't necessary. We made up the bed in the back and so one drove and the other two slept. How we needed that sleep. Carel drove just about all night, it worried me because he was already overtired. He really drove that Kombi – we would never have got to Wadi Halfa if he had not pushed the Kombi so. The desert was much harder here and we hit quite a few rocks, but fortunately no damage to the Kombi. Woke as dawn broke to find that we still had 70 miles to do. We all hoped that there would be no more pushing or else we would miss the steamer. It soon got hot, we were so dirty that all I wanted to do was jump in the Nile. Saw the Nile again just after 7 am then we knew Wadi Halfa was not very far away. Arrived in Wadi Halfa just after 10 am to find the Steamer waiting for us. Laugh, what panic when they found they still had to load the Kombi. I think just about all the officials helped to get us through Customs and Immigration. The Kombi took some loading, about 20 men all directing Carel. I was sure the darn thing would land in the Nile the way they carried on. Finally got on the Steamer just on 11:20 am and what a relief. The first thing we did was to shower and put clean clothes on, marvellous feeling. I had a cabin to myself and the boys shared the one next to mine. Very comfortable each with an electric fan. Went to lunch, how we enjoyed it as we had no breakfast. I slept in the afternoon. Carel went into the Abu Simbel Temples. I missed it as I was sleeping but I saw the carved entrance, a real marvel of rock carving. Wrote letters while the boys serviced the car. Had a beer before dinner, dinner and then to sleep – oh joy.

Ramp for Kombi, Waidi

Loading Kombi, Waidi

In a letter to Audrey, Joan writes the following account of the days since they parted and the hardship of the desert crossing which her diary entry does not entirely encapsulate.

"On Board the Nile Steamer
27th February, 1958

Dear Audrey,

Well as you can see we made it – but what a trip!! Definitely the worst we have struck so far. The poor old Kombi – how she struggled. But once again by sheer determination and brute force we arrived at Wadi Halfa 2 hours before the Steamer departed. Mind you they were waiting for us so it was a good thing that we had booked our passages.

Hope you had a good trip over and that you have managed to fix yourself up. Needless to say we all thought and talked about you most of Monday evening. It was a very sober trans African car that left Khartoum on the Monday evening.

For about the first 2 hours no one said very much – the silence was deadly. What a job getting out of Khartoum. It was dark by the time we crossed the bridge and as per usual there were no sign boards so the battle started early!! The first town we came to took us ¾ of an hour to get out of. Again, there were about 10 different roads all going the same way. We travelled until 1 am when the clutch cable broke so we just camped down there in the middle of the desert. For once we didn't have all the fuss and bother of looking for a camp spot!!! We slept until dawn. I did breakfast and the boys started putting in the new cable. How they struggled. We didn't move on until 11:15 am and was it hot just sitting out there in the middle of nowhere. After we got started we soon got stuck again this time in very soft sand. What a battle we had to unload the petrol, water and food box – it makes a big difference when there are only 2 pushing. We even let the tyres down to 10 lbs in front and 15 lbs in the back – must say it helped a lot but wrecked the tyres. Still they were the old ones so it didn't really matter. Most of Tuesday we travelled getting stuck about once an hour. We travelled slowly so we had to travel through the night. At 2:10 am on Wednesday morning we got so stuck that we decided to sleep until dawn. How we needed that sleep – we were all dead from heat, pushing and dirty sand. Well our luck was in because shortly after dawn while we were still struggling to get ourselves mobile again a truck arrived on the scene. He towed us out – I doubt if we would have managed on our own. After this we travelled together and what a good thing. The truck was fitted with desert tyres yet he seemed to gets struck in the soft sand as much as we did. Just after 1 pm we were joined by 2 more trucks (buses) so that now instead of one Kombi to push we had 3 trucks as well. It was wonderful as we had enough man power. We worked out quite a system eventually and managed to get ourselves unstuck quite quickly. We reached Abu Hamad just on sunset and filled up with petrol and water and set off under the direction of a police truck which was to going to Station Ten. The road from Abu Hamad to Wadi Halfa runs next to the railway line and if it hadn't been for that we would have lost the way. This stretch of road was much better – hard sand and we managed to keep going all night. Again Carel drove nearly all night – it worried me quite a bit because he hadn't slept well since Sunday night in Khartoum, Well we finally arrived in Wadi Halfa just before 10 am to find the Steamer waiting for us!!! What a good thing we had booked our passages. What fun – we were rushed through Customs and Immigrations and packed onto the boat with the help of nearly every official at Wadi Halfa. What a relief to be on the boat. We showered and went into the lunch and then slept. How we needed it – the most we could have slept in the 3 ½ days was about 9 hours. We must have made a nice picture – unwashed and shaved since leaving Khartoum!! Anyway we are really going to enjoy a bit of luxury on board the Steamer. We are very comfortable indeed. I have a cabin to myself and the boys are sharing the one next door. This is just the life.

Port Said
11th March, 1958

Yes you can well wonder why we are here. We are trying to get an earlier passage than the 20/3/58. What a job. We arrived in Cairo on the 5/3/58 after a wonderful 2 ½ days sightseeing at Luxor. Cairo is a wonderful place but expensive. We met an Egyptian family and they were very nice to us but you can't camp on people for too long. We have booked on the Corinthia leaving Alex on the 20/3/58. But we have been trying to get something sailing earlier but no go. We arrived here yesterday from Cairo just to get the same answer – most of the cargo ships don't stop at Port Said. So as soon as I have finished and posted this we are leaving for Alex to wait for the 20th. It is a darned nuisance because we have had enough of Egypt. I haven't time now to go into any more detail as Carel wants to get moving – we are parked right outside the Port Said Post Office.

By the way many thanks for your letter and the trouble you took finding out about shipping. I hope you have managed to track down some of the Angelis family by now – it will save you quite a bit of money. We seem to have spent masses here in Egypt – I can see us making a wild dash for London. I have had no letters from home as yet – hope there will be some in Athens. So until we meet on the 22/3/58 bye. The boys send their regards – look after yourself.

As ever, Joan
P.S. Carel has just gone off to see about some waters so I'll add a bit. Cairo was wonderfully decorated – celebrating the Union of the Arabic Republic. We spent one evening running and walking about the city streets – it was absolutely marvellous. We have also eaten quite a few Egyptian dishes which were most delicious.
P.S.S. We missed the boat on the 6th – we had a slight accident and got held up. Will give you more details in Athens, but we now have another cracked windscreen."

Joan's letter to Audrey

On board the Nile Steamer.
27th February, 1958.

Dear Audrey, Well as you can see we made it – but what a trip!! Definitely the worst we have struck so far. The poor old Kombi – how she struggled. But once again by sheer determination & brute force we arrived at Wadi Halfa 2 hours before the steamer departed. Mind you they were waiting for us so it was a good thing that we had booked our passages.

Hope you had a good trip over & that you have managed to fix yourself up. Needless to say we all thought & talked about you most of Monday evening. It was a very sober Trans African Co. that left Khartoum on Monday evening. For about the first 2 hours no one said very much – the silence was deadly. What a job getting out of Khartoum. It was dark by the time we crossed the bridge & as per usual there were no sign posts so the battle started early!! The first town we came to took us 1½ of an hour to get out of. Again there were about 10 different roads all going the same way. We travelled until 1 a.m when the clutch cable broke so we just camped down there – in the middle of the desert. For once we didn't have all the fuss & bother of looking for a camp spot!!! We slept until dawn. I did breakfast & the boys started putting in the new cable. How they struggled. We did move on until 11.15 a.m & was that just sitting out there in the middle of nowhere. After we got started we soon got stuck again. This time in very soft sand. What a battle we had to unload the petrol, water & food tins – it makes a big difference when there are only 2 pushing. We even let the tyres down to 10 lbs in front & 15 lbs in the back – must say it helped a lot but wrecked the tyres. Still they were the old ones so it didn't really matter. Most of Tuesday we travelled getting stuck about once an hour. We travelled slowly so we had to travel right through the night. At 2.10 a.m on Wednesday morning we got so stuck that we decided to sleep until dawn. How we needed that sleep – we were all dead from heat, pushing & dirty sand. Well our luck was in because shortly after dawn while we were still struggling

2.

to get ourselves mobil again a truck arrived on the scene. He towed us out – I doubt if we would have managed on our own. After this we travelled together & what a good thing. The truck was fitted with desert tyres yet he seemed to get stuck in the soft sand as much as we did. Just after 1 p.m we were joined by 2 more trucks (buses) so that now instead of 1 Kombi to push we had 3 trucks as well. It was wonderful as we had enough man power. We worked out quite a system eventually & managed to get ourselves unstuck quite quickly. We reached Abu Hamed just on sunset, filled up with petrol & water & set off under the direction of a police truck which was going to station on the road from Abu Hamed to Wadi Halfa – runs next to the railway line & if it hadn't been for that we would have lost the way. This stretch of road was much better – hard sand & we managed to keep going all night. Again Carl drove nearly all night – it worried me quite a bit because he hadn't slept well since Sunday night in Khartoum. Well we finally arrived in Wadi Halfa just before 10 a.m to find the steamer waiting for us!! What a good thing we had booked our passages. What fun – we were rushed through Customs & Immigration & packed onto the boat with the help of nearly every official at Wadi Halfa. What a relief to be on the boat. We showered & went into lunch & then slept. How we needed it – the most we could have slept in the 3 days was about 4 hours. We must have made a [illegible] picture – unwashed & unshaved since leaving Khartoum!! Anyway we are really going to enjoy a bit of luxury on board the steamer. We are very comfortable indeed. I have a cabin to myself & the boys are sharing the one next door. This is just the life.

Port Said.

11th March, 1958.

So you can well wonder why we are here. We are trying to get an earlier passage than the 20/3/58. What a job. We arrived in Cairo on the 5/3/58 after a wonderful 2 days sight-seeing at Luxor. Cairo is a wonderful place but expensive. We met an Egyptian family & they were very nice to us but you can't [illegible] on people for too long. We have booked on the Corinthia leaving Alex. on the 20/3/58. But we have been trying to get something sailing earlier but no go. We arrived here yesterday from Cairo just to get the same answer – most of

3

the cargo ships don't stop at Port Said. So as soon as I have finished & posted this, we are leaving for Alex to wait for the 20th. It is a darned nuisance because we have had enough of Egypt. I haven't time now to go into any more details as Carol wants to get moving – we are parked right outside the Port Said Post office.

By the way many thanks for your letter & the trouble you took finding out about shipping. I hope you have managed to track down some of the Angelus family by now – it will save you quite a bit of money. We seem to have spent masses here in Egypt – I can see us making a wild dash for London. I have had no letters from home as yet – hope there will be some in Athens. So until we meet on the 22/3/58 bye. The boys send their regards – look after yourself.

As ever,
Joan

P.S. Carol has just gone off to see about some water so I'll add a bit. Cairo was wonderfully decorated – celebrating the Union of the Arab Republic. We spent one evening driving & walking about the city streets – it was absolutely marvellous. We have also eaten quite a few Egyptian dishes which were most delicious.

J.

P.P.S. We missed the boat on the 6th – we had a slight accident & got held up. Will give you more details in Athens – but we now have another cracked wind-screen.

J.

Friday, 28th February 1958

Up almost as soon as it was light. Felt marvellous after my first night's decent sleep in four days. Did some washing and then showered. Went up on the top deck to read. It was very cool and peaceful up there. The Nile has broadened out to almost twice the size it was at Wadi Halfa. It is quite blue in colour here. Plenty of villages along the bank built on the rock, all the houses have flat roofs. We went into breakfast which we enjoyed. The service on the Steamer is very good. Wrote letters and read on the top deck. Carel and I took a lot of photos. Saw some native Nile boats, they all have the Arab dhow rigging and are very picturesque. The Nile flows through rocky gorges just before reaching Aswam. Had lunch onboard the ship. Arrived in Shellal while we were in the dining room, rushed to pack the car. As soon as the Steamer docked the Egyptian Immigration officials came onboard. I've never seen such chaos before. Everyone was shouting and running around in circles. Carel did all the paperwork thank goodness. I just sat looking after the cameras and loose bits and pieces. Had a bit of trouble getting the car off, too many directing Carel. They argue and fight amongst themselves quite a lot. Carel bought some very nice tomatoes at Shellal. Travelled into Aswan about 22 miles away. As it was the Arabic Sunday everything was closed. Drove around and had a look at the Cataract, where Carel gave some kids a hiding for throwing earth at the Kombi, he was really mad. Had a look at the Aswan Dam. It was very hot. While the boys filled up with petrol I watched a soccer match. The Egyptians play a very hard game, don't know how they do it in the heat. Drove about 15 miles out of Aswan and camped. We got another flat tyre, while the boys were mending it a lorry stopped and the driver helped the boys service the car while I cleaned up the desert dust and cooked our evening meal. It was so nice to be clean again. Quite a few passers-by came to say hello, but we couldn't understand them.

Saturday, 1st March 1958

Up early, it was quite chilly. Here in Egypt you have to drive on the right-hand side of the road. I started driving again and must admit that it was strange, seemed like the wrong side of the road. We travelled with the Nile on our left for about 50 miles through heavily cultivated land. The crops are so green alongside the stark desert on the right-hand side of the road. The people seem very poor but they work hard. Passed many of the old water pumps. They are very picturesque and working very well even if they are slow. After about 50 miles we veered to the right leaving the Nile to travel through the desert. At least it was a hard desert. It was very hot and we all felt it. Arrived in Luxor just before 3 pm, quite a big city. Everyone seems to walk in the middle of the road, you have to drive on your hooter. Went to the Tourist Bureau to find out about camping. Met an American girl and a Canadian girl there who are travelling North Africa on a scooter. Took them for tea, they were most interesting. The tourist officer found us a camp spot in the grounds of ex-King Farouk's Wills palace. After supper I washed some things. Marius went inside and Carel and I talked and talked. Things came to a head and he proposed to me – I was very happy and hope it will work but we have many difficulties to overcome. Went to bed well after 2 am.

Sunday, 2nd March 1958

Up early to be at the tourist office at 8 am to meet our guide for the day. Crossed the Nile in an Egyptian Dhow, the oarsmen sang as they rowed. On the West bank four donkeys were waiting for us. What fun we had getting on them. Surprisingly comfortable. Travelled about three miles touring the tombs in the Valley of the Kings. Temple of Deir el-Bahari, the Ramesseum, Valley of the Queens, Temple of Medinet Habu and the Colossi of Memnon. It was just too much to take in one go as we walked or climbed from the Valley of the King to Deir el-Bahari. We had an excellent guide called Bob and he really looked after us. Crossed the Nile again at 1:10 pm and had lunch in the Kombi parked alongside the Nile. Met Bob at 2:30 pm again and went to see the Temple of Karnak. Bob made it all so interesting, and showed us where to take the best photos. What an inspiring place. After Karnak we watch a modern procession of dancing, horse riding and stick playing. Bob took us into the mosque to hear the Quran being read. Very interesting, but strange. We were given Turkish tea by the priest at the Mosque, very tasty. Camped very late.

Carel, Joan and Marius on the donkey ride

Carel, Joan and Marius on the River Nile

Joan in front of the Temple of Hatshepsut

Joan and the Temple of Karnak

Joan and Carel, lane of Sphinx, Temple of Luxor

Carel, Joan and Marius, Valley of Kings

Monday, 3rd March 1958

Up early, it was lovely as we were camped right on the Eastern Bank of the Nile. It was a bit chilly, but the river looked terrific. Bob had invited us to his house for breakfast so after early morning coffee we broke camp. Met Bob parked the car and walked to his house. A very clean house. Had breakfast by ourselves Bob sat and talked to us. Ate omelette and homemade bread. I drank mint tea. It was very nice. Bob had a lovely Persian carpet draped over a settee. After breakfast he took us to see pottery being made. It was most interesting. The bank in Luxor would not cash our traveller's cheques so Carel had to cash some of his American dollars. Left Luxor just after 10 am and travelled about 190 miles north. The road was very crowded with Egyptians. They just walk anywhere on the road herding donkeys, camels and cattle. They never turn a hair when you blow the hooter, it is most exasperating. Why more of them don't get killed I don't know. We travelled on the east bank of the Nile. The land is very heavily cultivated – sugar cane, wheat, vegetables, plenty of tomatoes, Lucerne. It looked so nice the green land with the yellow dessert in the background. Plenty of date palms. They rear a lot of water buffalos for the milk and cream. I was tired but only managed to sleep for a short while, all the hooting kept me awake. We camped down for the night alongside one of the Nile canals. A very nice spot. While I was preparing our supper a car stopped and the driver told us it was dangerous for us to stay there. We didn't want to believe him because we were so comfortable, but then a whole crowd of Egyptians rolled up and they told us the same story. Had a bit of trouble with them and Carel nearly got into a fight. Packed up and while we were doing so a bus stopped and a policeman came to our rescue. He travelled with us to Asyut. Carel and I managed another get together while Marius was driving us to Asyut. We both needed it, the wait is going to be murder. The police in Asyut told us where to stay the night, but we pleased ourselves and we all slept in the Kombi parked in a field.

Asyut, Egypt

Tuesday, 4th March 1958

Woke early and dressed. We were parked in the middle of some lands. The farmer and his children rolled up to watch us. I gave him some coffee and then he gave us some eggs and water, a very nice gesture. After breakfast we went into Asyut for petrol and fresh produce. A very big city where the street scene was most interesting. Left Asyut just after 9 am, there is tarmac from Asyut to Cairo but we couldn't travel at more than 30 mph because the road was bumpy. Travelled along the east canal of the Nile, it is heavily cultivated land on either side of the road. The Egyptians seem to travel down the middle of the road and don't move their animals or themselves until you are just about to run them over.

Driving through the very numerous villages was an absolute nightmare. They seem to have very little road sense. While I was driving through a place called Ishment a fellow walked out from the side – walked right into the Kombi and I hit him. Fortunately for him and me I was only doing about 25 mph. I never even managed to break or swerve as he stepped out so suddenly. As soon as I stopped a huge crowd gathered and everyone was shouting at once. The fellow was lying where the car had flung him and he looked dead to me. I got such a shock that I couldn't even get out and help him. Carel tried to tell the crowd to fetch the police, but trouble started and he lost two buttons off his shirt. A policeman arrived and told us to move the car to the police station. I didn't want to but the crowd was getting quite nasty so Marius said move. At the police station the Captain in charge did a report and then called in two witnesses who gave a report and then I wrote out a report. What a business, Carel was wonderful and really helped me a lot. From Ishment we travelled with a policeman to Beni Suef to the police station[16]. Had to wait there for a report from the hospital about the chap. I was very worried and tired, everyone was talking but we couldn't understand them. They let us sleep in the first aid building after supper.

---

16 *With all the aggression going on my dad was thrown into jail until the situation was explained. The three were kept under police custody that night until the following day when it was established that the pedestrian's injuries were minor AND they had a court ruling allowing them to proceed.*

Joan's written report of the incident

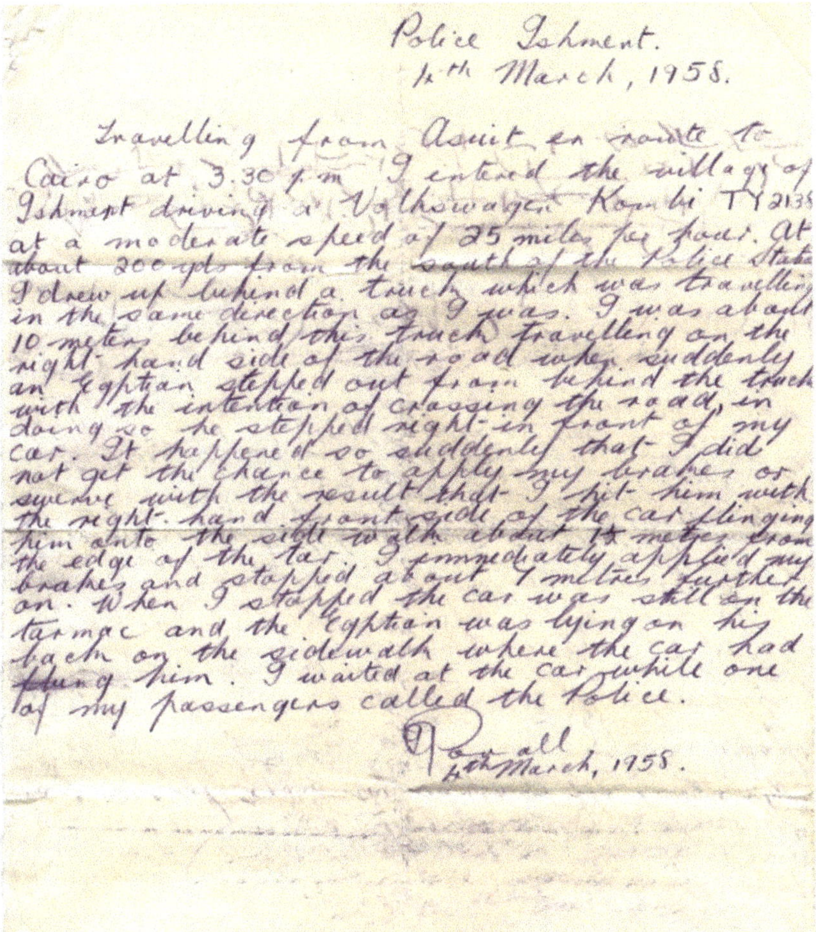

Police Ishment.
4th March, 1958.

Travelling from Asuit en route to Cairo at 3.30 p.m. I entered the village of Ishment driving a Volkswagen Kombi TY2135 at a moderate speed of 25 miles per hour. At about 200 yds from the south of the Police Station I drew up behind a truck which was travelling in the same direction as I was. I was about 10 meters behind this truck travelling on the right hand side of the road when suddenly an Egptian stepped out from behind the truck with the intention of crossing the road, in doing so he stepped right in front of my car. It happened so suddenly that I did not get the chance to apply my brakes or swerve with the result that I hit him with the right hand front side of the car flinging him onto the sidewalk about 15 meters from the edge of the tar. I immediately applied my brakes and stopped about 7 metres further on. When I stopped the car was still on the tarmac and the Egptian was lying on his back on the sidewalk where the car had flung him. I waited at the car while one of my passengers called the Police.

J Powall
4th March, 1958.

Wednesday, 5th March 1958 (Take Daraprim)

I woke early after a restless night. I was worried about the state of the fellow. He hadn't regained consciousness last night. After we had bathed and eaten our breakfast Marius and I went with a policeman to the hospital. About 30 beds with a resident doctor, the nurses were very casual and wore a loose white gown and no veil. The chap was alright, had a badly bruised nose and forehead. I was never more pleased to see anyone than this fellow. After the police officer had taken a statement from him, we were shown around the hospital and then taken back to the station. From the station we were taken to the court where a court official examined all the papers and asked a few questions. By this time the strain was taking its toll on me, but I was lucky and after giving us tea at the station they let us proceed to Cairo. Hope that will be the end of that. We travelled on to Cairo and arrived just before 1 pm. We wanted money but the banks were closed. What a place Cairo, much bigger than Joburg. The traffic was a real nightmare, everyone seemed to go his own way and the numerous policemen on point duty really battled. Went to the SA Legation for post and met Vernon Stuart the first Secretary. He told us quite a bit about Cairo and invited us to stay with him at his flat. We took up his offer. Parked the car in central Cairo and walked around looking for a ship booking to Athens. Seems like we are going to wait until the 20/3/58 to get a boat. Poor Audrey is going to have a long wait. Went to Vernon's flat just after 6 pm, had a drink with him and then a hot bath and hair wash. It was terrific. I really enjoyed it. He took us out for supper to the Pension where he normally eats. Had a very nice meal, met some of his friends, an American chap, an Egyptian girl and an English chap. Sat talking over a beer until 11 pm. Walked back to his flat. I slept in a bed for the first time since leaving the Union.

Thursday, 6th March 1958

Woke early and wrote letters. Vernon went to work and left us to get up. Had breakfast at the flat which I cooked and then we went into Cairo. Met Diedi, our Egyptian Medical Student friend, at the SA Legation and left the Kombi there. Diedi drove us around in his car, a good thing as it gave Carel the chance to look around too. The Cairo traffic is terrible, everyone drives on their hooters and the jaywalking is something to be seen to be believed. We parked the car and walked through the Musky. It was amazing and so interesting. Watched the gold and silversmiths working, a craft handed down by father to son. Walked along the Khan (the street of gold where all the Goldsmiths work). Went to a café and had green tea, a mint black tea which I really enjoyed. The streets of Cairo are really fascinating. Diedi took us back to the SA Legation at 2 pm where we picked up a guide that Vernon had arranged for us. He showed us around the Citadel and the old Mosques. The first one, the Mosque of Mohammed Ali was beautiful with the most glorious chandelier and Persian carpets. The tomb of Mohammed Ali is all inlaid in gold and ivory. Glorious view of Cairo from the Mosque. Next, we visited the Mosque of Sultan Hassan, the royal family Mosque, all the royal kings and queens etc are buried there. This Mosque they call the Blue Mosque because the ceiling is worked in blue marble, gold and ivory. It was breath-taking and must have cost a small fortune. I never dreamed that such work could be put into marble carving. The tomb of King Farouk's grandfather is engraved marble inlaid with ebony, ivory and gold. The last Mosque was the Mosque of Rifai and is one of the oldest in Cairo. It is not really decorated but there is a gold door in the Mosque which is 1300 years old. It is heavily barracked. I bought my marble Nefertiti for £1. What a wonderful afternoon. Dropped our guide in Opera Square and then tried to find Diedi but couldn't so we drove and then later walked around Cairo. The whole town was beautifully decorated as they are celebrating the formation of the Arabic Republic. Glorious sight with most buildings and bridges floodlit. Camped late in the quarry at Mokattam. Full moon and Cairo looked terrific from the Citadel.

Cairo city centre

Cairo

Friday, 7th March 1958

Carel and I had a late-night last night after Marius had gone to bed. We talked about us, it's not going to be easy but we both mean to make a success of our lives together. Neither of us want to wait long before getting married, seems as if we will marry shortly after arriving in England. I'm glad because Carel needs me as much as I need him. It was not what I planned before leaving home but then I'll only be happy with him nearby so the sooner the better – we've nothing to wait for really. We slept late, Carel mended a puncture and after a late breakfast we drove into Cairo. It was a terrible day, we couldn't see Cairo city from Mokattam, there was a desert wind blowing called "Khamsin" and everywhere we went we experienced the fine desert sand being blown around. Something like our berg wind at home, warm and dirty. Tried to fix up our boat to Greece but still can't find one before the 20th. The car wouldn't start after being parked outside the travel agency so Carel had to put on an overall and see what was wrong. While he was working, I wrote letters and Marius read, my, but he is lazy. He never does more than he can possibly help, makes me mad at times[17]. We had lunch in the car parked just outside the travel agency. It was nice as we had fresh butter, cheese and bread. So nice to get the fresh stuff. Drove around Cairo looking for camel chairs. I am sure Marius guessed our secret while Carel and I went buying the chairs, we wanted a pair and he just looked at us but said nothing. Bought some fresh vegetables and camped early again in the quarry at Mokattam. It was very unpleasant as the wind was blowing very hard and the desert dust was really something terrible. We ate a cold meal and went to bed early. I was very tired and slept like a log. I rubbed Carel's hair before going to sleep. He spoils me terribly but I love him so that's alright.

Saturday, 8th March 1958

Up very early, we had a lot to do. Applied for our Greek visas and got them within an hour. Tried the travel agency again for an earlier booking but still no go. They advised us to go to Port Said to see if we can catch a cargo steamer, we'll go tomorrow afternoon. Spent a long-time buying souvenirs. We got our camel chairs, Carel got Hermin's sent "Secret of the Moon", I got some slippers. Actually we had a good time in the shop just looking at everything. Went to the SA Consulate to say cheerio, sorry we won't see more of Vernon Stewart he's a very nice fellow. Went through the Cairo museum of Antiquities, a most marvellous collection. The old Egyptians certainly knew how to use gold, Tut Anila Amson treasures of gold were really terrific. Had tea just outside the museum, the guides worried us a lot. Met Diedi at 5 pm and he took us to watch some Egyptian folklore dancing which he does. It was really very interesting, the music a little strange but it grew on me. All played on a small drum and the rest was sung. Met some other Egyptians and after the dancing we went to Prof and Mrs Hassan Tapnois house for tea. They had a lovely home, a big flat on the 7th floor of a building in Heliopolis, a suburb of Cairo. Saw some colour slides then we young folk went out to eat Egyptian food. It was really delicious and we all enjoyed it, a bit rich but very tasty. Went to a show of belly dancing at 12:05 am,

---

[17] *I feel the need to defend my Uncle and present another facet to him. Marius was a very clever (he did exceptionally well on the South African stock market), but soft spoken, quiet, reserved person who remained a bachelor his whole life. In his 60s he was asked to stand as guarantor on a student loan for the daughter of a friend of my dad's. Never having met her he simply wrote out a cheque there and then for the full cost of the course, a 4-year legal degree. He insisted he did not want to be paid a penny back, but said to her if she was ever in a position to help someone to do so. He had a good and generous heart!*

no one seem to consider time in Egypt. Enjoyed the show, drank sugar cane juice afterwards and then went to Diedi's home to spend the night with him. I had a room to myself and the boys were together next door, slept like a log.

Sunday, 9th March 1958

Woke early, had a shower and breakfast. Ate Egyptian food for breakfast – beans and arbanheit and milk porridge, it was very tasty. Fetched Hilga, Diedi's girlfriend, and then went out to the Pyramids at Giza. It was very hot and I was very surprised at the rough surfaces of the Pyramids. Walked around outside took some photos and then went inside. What a climb, fantastic to think of it as a burial chamber. Had a beer at the restaurant next to the Pyramids. Drove back to Cairo where Diedi took us around and we bought provisions and then went to tea at the house. It was lovely there; a beautiful day and we sat out on the stoep and watch the horse racing seven storeys below. After tea, Diedi showed us the way out of Cairo to Port Said. Travelled until 5:30 pm and then camped alongside a canal. Did some washing.

Sphinx

Monday, 10th March 1958

Woke early, travelled on to Ismailia where we first saw the Suez Canal. Ismailia is a big town situated along the canal, very beautiful. The canal is so blue, shockingly so, also it's not as wide as I thought it would be. We were very lucky in meeting a convoy of over 30 ships travelling south, they looked so quaint, big ships in the middle of the desert. We took some photos contrary to the police regulations, no harm meant really but we had to have a few shots of the Kombi alongside the Canal. The Suez Canal road is in excellent condition and runs all along the canal, stopped for tea, it was very pleasant. Arrive in Port Said just before lunch, went to see the shipping agents and then drove around. The town is spread along the seafront which is not particularly clean. Went out to the Port Said aerodrome to use the toilet and found an aeroplane crash. The wreck was very heavily guarded by policemen, laugh, we had quite a job getting into the aerodrome building – were met at the door by a guard carrying a great big air-cooled rifle. But by this time my need was too great and I just barged on with Carel at my heels. When the guard saw what my idea was, he laughed and called for the key. Driving back to the city centre we found a very nice camp spot right on the beachfront. Walked about the city and the curio shops. We spent quite a bit of money on leather goods. I managed to persuade Carel to accept a leather lounger jacket. Quite an achievement really. The streets of Port Said were really very interesting but we were pestered a bit by guards. Just about the whole of Port Said is an army, they simply teem all over the place. The whole beachfront is closed off and there were some big guns. Parked right on the beach. Egypt is certainly getting prepared for something; Nasser is definitely very unsure of his position. I have never seen so many policemen round the streets. Went back to our camp spot pitched camp and I did a lot of washing. We were nearly eaten by the flies and as soon as it was dark the mosquitoes started. Didn't sleep very well on account of the mosquitoes.

Carel and Marius, Port Said

Tuesday, 11th March 1958

We were woken very early by a police officer. He was in a great big black Chevy car and escorted by two policemen carrying guns big enough to blast us and the Kombi off the face of the earth. It was really very funny but frightening. Carel dealt with him, he checked our passports and then gave us permission to spend another day at our camp. I did some washing while Carel did breakfast. He is a dear, wish Marius would take a leaf out of his book. Waited for the washing to dry and then went into Port Said to hear whether Phynos had managed to get us a passage. No go so it means travelling back to Cairo and confirming our booking for the 20/3/58 and then travelling on to Alexandria. We were all disappointed. Left Port Said just after 12 pm, stopped for tea along the Suez Canal. It was very pleasant, a lovely breeze blowing off the Canal. The only thing that marred it was the presence of an armed policeman who looked at us most suspiciously the whole time we were parked. They are a very suspicious crowd. Travelled on and camped down about 50 miles out of Cairo alongside one of the Canals. I did some washing which blew dry very quickly. Had supper and went to bed shortly after 8 pm. At 9:45 pm we were awakened by someone banging on the back of the Kombi. Carel got up to find another policeman investigating our presence. What a business, he wanted us to break up camp and go with him to the police station. Carel was getting really cross and managed to persuade him that he would go with him to the police station if we could leave the Kombi camped where it was. Well he took our passports and was away until 12:30 am. I nearly went mad. I lay imagining all kinds of things, Marius slept through it all. I have never spent such an anxious 2½ hours and never want it repeated. When Carel returned alright I nearly burst into tears. Apparently, he met a doctor and army captain at the police station and they had kept him talking[18].

Joan alongside the Suez Canal

---

[18] *My dad was arrested as a suspected spy, taken to the military camp and interrogated by the Capitan. It started very aggressively but he managed to diffuse the situation, ending up in an arm wrestle, which he strategically lost. The air cleared, the Capitan opened a bottle of wine & they proceeded to chat like old friends until the bottle was finished. He was eventually returned to the campsite with permission to temporarily camp in the Military Zone.*

Wednesday, 12th March 1958 (Take Daraprim)

Woke early after a night I never want to repeat. After breakfast Carel took Marius and I to meet the doctor. Laugh, I was introduced as his fiancé just to overcome all difficult explanations. Laugh, I've been demoted, I was his wife last week!!! We sat and talked to the doctor and ate oranges and drank tea. The doctor shouted a bit and never stopped talking, my ears just buzzed. After leaving them we continued on our way to Cairo. Went straight to the SA Legation to see Vernon Stewart. Made a date for the evening and then took the car into a Shell garage to have the oil changed. Walked around central Cairo bought a pair of sandals. Went and parked the Kombi alongside the Nile on the western bank and had lunch. The fountains in the middle of the Nile were working and it was a lovely sight, wrote letters. Went back to town and visited the Musky. We parked the car and walked around. It was really fascinating to watch the various craftsmen working. It is quite an art to walk in the streets of the Musky. All the shopkeepers call you into their shops saying, "You don't have to buy, just look around". They are all excellent salesmen so one has very little chance, really. The streets teem with people, donkey carts, cars and you have to battle your way through. The noise is almost deafening as everyone shouts and the car hooters never stop, I nearly had heart failure much to Carel's amusement. Went back to Vernon's (Jim's) flat for supper. Jim was out so I cooked supper while the boys washed and then I bathed. It was so nice lying in a bath of hot water. When Jim came back at 9 pm we went to the flick. His girlfriend, Kirsty, a Danish lass who works in the Danish Embassy, went with us. She spoke good English with an American accent. We saw Sanayou, not bad, a very big theatre, came out at 12:45 am and then we went for coffee!! Went back to Jim's flat packed up and travelled out of Cairo and camped about 10 miles out on the Alexandria Road. We were all very sleepy. It was cold.

Thursday, 13th March 1958

Woke at approximately 4:30 am when the wind blew the tent loose. We were camped in the desert sand and the sand wasn't firm enough to hold the pegs. The whole tent was flapping. Carel got up but couldn't manage so I got out and helped him. The wind "Khamsin" was very strong and bitterly cold. I only had my pyjamas and a jersey on and I nearly froze. We battled to tie the flaps down. By the time we were finished we were both nearly frozen. Marius didn't move a finger to help, as per usual. Sometimes his laziness really gets to me. Carel climbed in the Kombi with me and we warmed each other up then he got in his own bed. I'm so glad and happy that I have got him, only hope we won't have to wait too long once we get to London to get married. It will mean a struggle to start off, but we both feel that together we will manage. Further than that we haven't a clue at present. We packed up early and set off along the desert road to Alexandria. A very good road, tarmac, right across the desert sand, an amazing feat really. It was very hot and dusty. During the day the Khamsin wind becomes a hot wind and it is most unpleasant. The sand was being blown across the road and we had to keep all our windows shut. I felt awful, had a headache and slept the time at the back. We arrived in Alex just after 3 pm, parked alongside the western coast and had tea and something to eat. The wind was still blowing and the sea was very rough. I got out of the car and climbed down the rocks to put my feet in the Mediterranean Sea. It was quite cold at about 68. Carel also climbed down but wouldn't get wet. After tea we drove into Alex and went to the Visitors Bureau to find a camp spot but they couldn't help us. I couldn't get out of the car as I had my jeans on. Wrote letters in the car while Carel went to see the shipping agents. Drove out of Alex on the eastern side, 10 miles of sea front, it looked so nice. Found a camp, wind still blowing cold, cooked in the car and we all slept in the car, much warmer that way.

Friday, 14th March 1958

Had breakfast where we were parked then drove a little further on and re-packed the Kombi. What a business as everything was upside down. Washed and dressed and then drove towards Alexandria. We stopped and went into one of the ex-King Farouk's palaces, El Montazah Palace. What a beautiful palace built right on the sea front and so tastefully laid out. At first only Carel and I went in and we walked around until we found a lovely summer house built on the rocks with sea all around – we wanted to take some photos so Carel left me sitting in the summer house while he fetched the Kombi and Marius. It was a perfect day and being Friday just about all Egypt and his wife were there, there was a very big group of students playing around. Farouk certainly knew how to pick a piece of land with a view. Carel and I walked all over the place. We parked the car so that we could have lunch in the sun. I made some tomato sandwiches and an Egyptian family got out and came and talked to us. They were all full of welcome and wanted to know all about our trip. We didn't really appreciate their visit as we were hungry and our tea was getting cold. They left just after 3 pm so we ate our sandwiches and drank our cold tea and drove into Alexandria. We went to the Tourist office. They advised us to go to the Scout Camp ground at Abu Qir (Aboukir), 18 miles west of Alexandria. The man in the office was very rude and insinuating, his types are no good in Tourist offices. We drove around Alex for a bit and then bought some fruit and vegetables and drove out to Abu Qir. We found the campground and the person in charge welcomed us and said we could pick our own spot. It's a very nice place and we have all conveniences very close. Abu Qir is the sweetest little fishing village but again heavily guarded by the army, very big guns in the sand dunes.

Alexandria

Saturday, 15th March 1958

Up early – breakfast, broke camp and motored into Alex. The sea front stretches for about 12 miles and is really terrific. The bathing booths at the swimming beaches are built one on top of the other – some are 5 and 6 together high. The sea looked most inviting – a glorious deep blue. I would like to swim before leaving Alex. Once in Alex we went to see the agents about our booking on the "Carinthia". To save money Carel and I have taken deck space only – hope it won't be too rough or cold for us. We are banking on being able to sleep in the Kombi. Marius is going 3rd class – hope he likes it for a change – he seems to be so darn fussy. Carel and I walked around quite a bit – it was most interesting. The only pity was that we had no spare cash to indulge in our whims. Bought groceries and then went and had lunch on the sea front right next to the Ras el Fin Palace – another of ex-King Farouk's mansions. Mind you, it's a pity that the Egyptian authorities didn't look after such priceless pieces, but they didn't care about Farouk's things. Watched a boy throwing a net like Garth did. He was getting very small sardines – I spent quite a while picking up shells – there were plenty. Drove back to Abu Qir – had supper and then wrote letters. The boys read until bedtime.

Sunday, 16th March 1958

Slept late, it was so nice. We are going to have a big clean up today so we felt we could afford the luxury of a lie in. It is very cold at night here, but the days are very hot. I spent just about all day washing Carel's and my dirty clothes, everything was very dirty. It soon dried in the warm wind. Ages since we have been so clean. Marius spent all day mending the torn roof canvas and Carel spent the day working on the car. Altogether we have a very successful day. Couldn't get rid of the gallery though. Carel and I managed another get together before going to bed.

Tobruk, Egypt

Monday, 17th March 1958

The mosquitoes nearly ate me alive last night, it's so funny to get them so close to the sea. We had another late sleep and really appreciated it. After breakfast Marius did his washing. I can't understand why he wouldn't let me do it, likes to be independent. I oiled my hair and sat and fixed Carel's trousers, he was working on the car again. Then he washed my hair for me, what a business but I enjoyed it. I washed his jerseys and his cardigans, all very dirty. Then we all had a break for lunch – I made a salad of onion, tomatoes and cabbage eaten with fresh bread; it was terrific. After lunch I finished off my own washing and then wrote some letters. Carel has got the windscreen wipers on the Kombi going again. He also fixed the lights. It is going to be so nice having someone around who can use his hands. I'm really going to appreciate this fact. We want to walk around a bit and explore Abu Qir but we are a bit scared of running into the army again. I haven't been sleeping well for the last few days. I keep getting giddy and having slight headaches due to my usual not arriving at all. Last month I had trouble and pain and now it hasn't happened at all. Carel is most concerned about me not being well. He cooked supper last night for me and Marius. Cooked it tonight. Very sweet of them both. Mind you they both turned out very good meals, Audrey and I will have to watch our steps in future. I got into bed and Carel rubbed my back for me. It was so nice. The boys read for quite a while then made themselves some tea before turning in. I honestly don't know what Marius thinks about all day, he never says much, he is a very colourless sort of person.

Tuesday, 18th March 1958

Had another late morning, I gave the boys breakfast in bed. After washing the dishes we broke camp and drove into Alex to fix our passages on the Carinthia. Marius fixed up the paying and Carel and I bought food. We found a shop which had a very nice assortment. Walked around the market looking for some dried dates and oranges. I was not feeling so well, very giddy at times. It was hot and I got very tired. Drove out of Alex and had a late lunch parked along the promenade. I made some tomato sandwiches which we ate with our tea sitting on the sea wall. It was very pleasant sitting in the sun. Watched a motorboat being off loaded from a ferry. Quite a tricky business. Drove back to Abu Qir and pitched camp. Marius stayed at the camp and Carel and I walked around Abu Qir exploring. It's quite a big town. We walked through the town and then around the Bay on the beach[19]. Spent quite a long time picking up shells – Carel and I teased each other – I was so happy. Found an old fort at the end of the bay and we walked all along the outer wall. The sea looked good enough to swim but we couldn't due to army regulations. We sat on the beach for quite a while talking about ourselves and our parents. Back at camp I started on supper. I was very tired and tried to get supper over and done with as quickly as possible. I got into bed early and Carel rubbed my back for me. I went to sleep long before the boys did. Think Carel is a bit worried over my health, time will cure it I am sure. I wonder what Marius thinks of the whole business, he must guess a certain amount but up to now he's said nothing.

---

19 *At one point while walking on the beach (my dad had his camera slung over his shoulder) a soldier approached them, pulled his gun out, pointed it at them, cocked it and accused them of being British spies. My dad managed to talk him down and they carried on walking, but it was a very tense moment for a while.*

Thursday, 20th March 1958

Up very early – breakfast. Packed the car in preparations for the over sea voyage to Piraeus. Drove into Alexandria and arrived at the docks just before 9:30 am. We were met by the Egyptian A.A. officials and they helped us through the Customs and Immigration. What a business, they were full of nonsense. Anyway by 11:30 am we reached the dockside where the Carinthia was berthed. They were very busy loading bananas and tomatoes and we had to wait. Well we waited until after 3 pm to be told that they had passages for us but not for the car. We were furious. Poor old Audrey is going to have a longer wait than we expected. The Hellenic Mediterranean Lines offered us a passage for ourselves and the Kombi on the M.S. Lydia is sailing tomorrow. It will be a round trip to Limassol in Cyprus, Beirut, Port Said, Alexandria and then Piraeus. Well we got so sick of the Egyptians and the way they did things that we decided to take the round trip at the company's expense. So we watched them finish loading the Carinthia and then we watched her sail. I was very upset, I wasn't feeling well and I was most disappointed. Anyway, perhaps it was for the good that we were left behind. So Carel fixed up with the police and Immigration and we camped on the docks. I'm sure we created history because everyone seemed to know about us. I tried to sleep a bit but the flies got me down. Marius wasn't feeling so well and got sick just before supper. After supper, Carel and I walked around the docks. Again, we had to be careful where we walked because of the police and army guards. All in all, we had a nice interesting walk – there were a lot of Dutch, German and Danish cargo boats in the harbour. We even managed to have a long chat about ourselves. Carel wanted to get a job in England and then in about three months' time we'll get married. I think we are going to have a bit of a battle trying to get everything straightened out. We all slept in the Kombi, I wasn't so well.

Friday, 21st March 1958

Up early, Carel made coffee as I wasn't feeling so well. Broke camp and then parked on the dockside where the Lydia was to dock. What a day, the wind was blowing great guns and it was very cold. We are in for a very rough voyage. It was very boring waiting. Many small ships came in and still we waited for the Lydia. She was expected at 9 am and she finally docked at 2:10 pm. Met a Greek man on the docks who knew South Africa very well. The A.A. man Attar, arrived shortly after the Lydia docked. He took all our papers again and left us sitting on the dockside. The ship was loading tomatoes. Marius boarded the ship first to stay with the car once it was loaded. Finally at 5:40 pm, they started loading the Kombi. What a business, they fitted a net around the front wheels and one around the back wheels then put the crane hook through both and lifted it up. My heart was in my mouth as she swung around in mid-air. Carel and I took some photos of the loading and then went on board. At first, they told us that there were no cabins for us so Carel set up a moan. He asked to see the shipping agent and then moaned to them. It had its results because we got our cabins. Not very good ones but at least somewhere to rest our heads. Very near the dining room. I was to share with two old ladies and a young girl and the boys were next door sharing with three old men. We went into supper after the ship had sailed, we were still in fairly calm water. After a good supper, we unpacked our things from the Kombi. Carel and I took a walk around the deck, checked up on how the Kombi was parked and then went to bed. The ship was just going up and down, but I managed to sleep.

Loading the Kombi

Saturday, 22nd March 1958

We were well out to sea when I woke and the boat was really rolling. There was a strong wind blowing and the sea was very choppy. I got up on very shaky legs and went up on the top deck. Carel joined me and we ate an orange before breakfast, a thing I shouldn't have done because it made me sick. I didn't eat much breakfast. Marius was feeling fine but Carel was not. As the day progressed, the weather got worse and the ship was rolling badly. I stayed up on deck with the boys but I was feeling like death warmed up. We arrived at Limassol, the Cyprus port, late in the afternoon. The sea was very rough and it was raining on and off. Due to the security regulations on Cyprus the British Occupied Forces boarded and searched the boat. We moored in the roadstead and they loaded and unloaded from barges. Gosh! But those sailors have to know their job. A lot of women and children refugees boarded the ship. Went to bed early feeling very sorry for myself. My legs were very sore.

Sunday, 23rd March 1958

The ship sailed during the early hours of the morning; I woke feeling awful. Decided to stay in bed, Carel brought me some biscuits to the cabin. The sea was still very rough and it was raining and the Lydia just rolled around and I rolled with it. I was not sick, but I had a headache and felt very giddy. Got up after lunch and sat right up front with the boys, still didn't feel so hot. The sea became very rough as we approached Beirut. Marius and I got wet up front while Carel was showering. All the refugees were sitting about the deck getting seasick, what a sight. I lay on my bunk as we went into Beirut. Got up for supper which we had in Beirut harbour. Wrote letters and went to bed early. Carel went into town with some other fellows.

Monday, 24th March 1958

Up for breakfast which I enjoyed as I was very hungry. They were very busy loading the ship. We had passes to leave the ship but it was raining so we waited for it to stop before leaving the ship. Carel and I wrote letters in the dining room. My legs were still aching like a cramp, but I decided to go into town thinking that the exercise would do them good. Walked up the main square where Carel changed some American dollars so that we could buy stamps for our letters. The streets of Beirut were very busy, something like Cairo. Everyone drives on their hooters and there seems to be more cars than people. We were struck by the number of big American cars on the roads. A very big city and very modern with plenty of café and sandwich stalls. The Lebanese are very fond of their food just like the Egyptian. We walked through the market where you could buy almost anything. Bought some very nice apples which we ate as we walked around. Some fellow in the street took us to see his curio shop. There were some very nice things for sale and much cheaper than the Egyptian stuff. But we had very little money so we couldn't buy. I would have loved to buy some silk Brocade but had to leave it. Carel bought a small heart inlaid coffee table for £5. He left Marius and I and went back to the ship for some more dollars. I was very tired and my legs were aching. I just wanted to go back to the ship but I had to wait. Carel joined us again and then we looked for tobacco for Marius. I was feeling very miserable. Carel bought me an Easter egg. Walked back to the ship. I rested and watched them loading. Went to bed very tired with aching legs.

Tuesday, 25th March 1958

Didn't sleep at all well, my legs were aching too much. Wish I knew what was wrong with them. Had changed cabins last night, a much better cabin that I shared with a mother and daughter. Got up, washed and dressed but my legs were aching so I lay down again. Carel came in to see me after breakfast and helped me up onto the deck. Once up there I felt much better. The one steward very kindly called Carel and gave him some rusks for me. Carel rubbed my legs and it helped a lot. Carel did some bookkeeping and I relaxed in the sun. After lunch we put a blanket out on the aft deck and lay in the sun. Carel gave me another massage and it helped relieve the pain, I wonder why my legs ache. We both had a nice sleep until some very noisy fellows came up on the aft deck and woke us. The sea was very calm and it was very pleasant sitting in the sun. Wrote letters up on the aft deck, burnt quite a bit. At about 4 pm we sighted land and went up on the far deck to watch the approach to Port Said. The pilot came out in a very big launch – we were very surprised when we found out that it was the pilot's launch, really big. Took us one hour to get into the harbour. It was getting chilly. Much yelling on board as a big party of Germans was disembarking to motor to Cairo. We tied up almost opposite de Lesseps' broken-down statue! What fun when all the vendors boarded the ship. They were all trying to get on quickly with the result that there was a tremendous amount of yelling. How we laughed. They had to load from small boats and everything seemed to go wrong. Anyway, they seemed to sell just about every chap, a new pair of shoes. Supper, then Carel and I talked quite a long while and off to bed.

Cruising the Mediterranean

Joan and Carel

Port Said and Kombi stored on board

Wednesday, 26th March 1958

Woke early to the sound of the ship being loaded, what a racket. Got up and went into breakfast. After breakfast I had a shower and washed my very dirty hair. Sat up on deck and dried my hair and typed my circular letter. Carel sat with me writing. The loading of the ship was taking much longer than they expected. What a racket they make. Had lunch and really enjoyed it, the first time for days!! We finally left Port Said at 12:40 pm. The sea was very calm and the most glorious blue. We had to battle to find a seat on the aft deck, too many people on board ship. We didn't get far out to sea, could see land all the way. Carel and I stood on the fore deck watching the sea just about all afternoon. The sea became very rough as we approached Alex. The wind was blowing great guns. Needless to say I went to bed straight after supper. They loaded the ship just about all night.

Thursday, 27th March 1958

Got up in time for breakfast. Nice to be able to eat meals. They loaded the ship all morning, what a business and such a row. People were boarding the ship all morning, I wonder where we are all going to fit in. Plenty of Germans, all for deck space. We were lucky enough to be left in our cabins. Carel and I wrote and typed letters all morning. After lunch we had a sleep. The wind got up and it was very cold. We left Alex after tea. The sea was very rough, sure I am going to be seasick. Had a wonderful view of ex-King Farouk's Palace, Ras-el Fin, as we left Alex. Also saw the Egyptian naval base and submarines. Passed by a big wreck, thought we were going to hit it. I didn't have supper, ship rolling too much, to bed early.

Friday, 28th March 1958

What a day, the sea was very rough and I spent most of the day in bed. Carel brought me breakfast and lunch. Lay on my bunk talking to the old lady in the cabin. Got up for a while just before tea but it was too much for me and I had to retire. Carel brought me an apple for supper and sat and talked to me. I did enjoy his company after a day by myself. He teased me a lot about being seasick but I don't mind – enjoy his company too much for that. Got into bed just before 10 pm. Hope the sea is calmer tomorrow for our arrival in Greece.

Saturday, 29th March 1958

Got up early and had a shower. The boat wasn't rolling so much and I felt much better. Went into breakfast which I enjoyed. Carel and I went up on deck. Saw land then enjoyed watching the islands as we sailed past. I'd like to explore them all in a small yacht, that's if I didn't get seasick. After seeing land we seemed to sail so slowly. We were itching to get to Piraeus. Finally arrived at 10:45 am, Audrey was on the quay to meet us. She was with a German girl whom she had met at the Y.W.C.A at Athens. Took us one hour to get through customs. We all went back to the Y.W.C.A for lunch – very cheap but good. Margaret Peters, the German girl, had lunch with us. Walked about Athens waiting for the shops to open. Their Easter decorations were really beautiful. Did some shopping, what a job trying to make ourselves understood. Can't say I care for the Greek shopkeepers, they are not very helpful. Left Margaret at the Y.W.C.A and travelled about 10 miles out of Athens. Had a wonderful time repacking all Audrey's and my clothes. How we two talked.

Offloading the Kombi in Piraeus, Greece

Sunday, 30th March 1958

Found Corinth and castle.

Joan and Carel in Athens, Greece

Athens, Greece

Monday, 31st March 1958

Acropolis, Visas, slept airport.

Marius, Audrey, Joan and Carel, the Acropolis

Camping spot in Athens

Tuesday, 1st April 1958

Athens, dinner at Busty's.

Audrey in Athens

South African Consulate, Athens

Wednesday, 2nd April 1958

As described by Audrey in her diary:

"In spite of going to sleep only at 2:00 am, got up at 6:30 and made coffee etc. A cold wind still blowing but the sun was warm when it rose. Had cold fish from Bastiaanse for breakfast. Got dressed and packed and left camp at 9:00 going first into Athens where I bought a little vase and found out about the carpets at Delphi. Joan and I bought food, giving great thought to cost, returned to the Kombi and drove out to SA Legation with Marius to say cheerio to Irene and Mr Bastiaanse. Returned to the Y.W.C.A to meet Carel and pick-up Margaret. Piled into the Kombi and went up to Mary's to find she had gastroenteritis. She saw the Kombi and we said cheerio and drove through the heavy traffic out of town in the direction of Delphi passing the churches of Daphne and Apollo. The sun was shining hotly and the countryside was much more beautiful than on Sunday last. We stopped for tea and sandwiches and drove on up into the mountains. I was thrilled at everything and so happy to be moving again. Saw ploughman standing on ploughs drawn by 2 horses, green wheat and blossoming almond trees. Later in the afternoon the scenery changed to grape farms and we were high in the mountains with a snow-capped peak ahead of us. Reached Delphi at about 7:30 in light rain and after enquiries carried on down the mountain again to the village where Margaret was to stay. Saw carpets in Delphi. Village very quaint and Kombi went down the narrowest street and up a stepped one. Left Margaret and camped above the village overlooking the sea. Had stew, all hungry but in spite of snow, not too cold."

Delphi camp spot

Delphi camp view

Thursday, 3rd April 1958

As described by Audrey in her diary:

"Woke to a beautiful misty view of the sea and snow-capped mountains. Had bread, butter and jam for breakfast and packed up to fetch Margaret by 8:30. Dressed in slacks and walking shoes, walked down the village street to find her waiting (having had a very primitive night!) and drove back to Delphi. Parked Kombi outside the museum and walked along to the old spiritual centre of Delphi. Saw the ruins of the treasure house, the temple votive statue base, the theatre and right high up, the arena. The sun was shining and the view across the mountains, beautiful. Margaret told us what she could, but even she was disappointed to find it so ruined. Saw lots of lovely poppies and fields of green corn. Returned to the Kombi, had coffee and bread etc for lunch, took photos. Margaret relaxed as never before I felt! Went to the other side of the road and the ruins and then returned in the Kombi to Delphi to buy my carpet. Got one for 65 drachmas and a little Evzones doll. Took Margaret back to camp and took some cine of the camp routine. Used the cine for the first time! Did washing, shoes all had chores to do to M's delight and then I used a tin of bully beef for supper to which persuaded M to stay. Carel and I walked her back to the house in the village, clear cold moonlight night and retired when we got back. Joan suffering somewhat from a sore throat."

Audrey, Joan, Carel and Marius in Delphi

Friday, 4th April 1958 (Good Friday)

As described by Audrey in her diary:

"Another lovely morning, got going early and onto the road, down through the village then across the country to the main road north. Beautiful mountainous country with the snow always just out of reach. Roads are winding and potholed, passing through little villages where the women wear nearly all black – very poor. Miles of wheat cultivation, horse ploughs, donkeys, grey green olive trees."

Saturday, 5th April 1958

As described by Audrey in her diary:

"Rose early at 6:30 to get breakfast, but Joan felt better and just stayed in bed for food. It was dull and the sun only shone a little as we drove on through some more mountainous country, above the mist once. The road improved and we got down to the plains, arrived in Salonika at about 12:30. Went to Stratigou. Doumpiotou and looked up George Barseltiden, arranged to meet him later and went off to look around the market and shops. Carel met him at about 4:00 about money exchange and having to wait 'till six we went to see the visiting Italian frigates. Saw their submarine but only from outside, it was very big and I was duly impressed. A young Italian showed us very nicely over the frigate which had television and a bicycle on it! The others found this contrast of freedom with Egypt amazing. Went to the fish market to buy a cheap meal! Found all the fish very expensive! But the fish market was an education. Completed the money business then went back along the road to the Yugoslavia turn off and camped in the dark just off the road. Marius is not spending his money as we are going quickly through Europe."

Sunday, 6th April 1958 (Easter)

Easter Sunday. Up very early to get breakfast ready before the boys woke. Audrey drew some pictures on our Easter eggs. We had some fun at breakfast time. Carel had bought us Easter eggs and we set the table and put them on. Marius didn't not join in the fun, sometimes I wish he were not with us, he's such a damper. Fancy being asked, "What's good about Easter". He has no imagination at all, poor fellow, he misses so much. We all enjoyed the boiled eggs, the first we have had for weeks. It was very cold, snow on the mountains. Travelled through a beautiful valley where the trees were just beginning to blossom. Had lunch in the sun on a grass bank. It was so nice. Arrived at Skopje, a very big place, took petrol. Got stuck in the snow water and also helped a Canadian out stuck in his Studebaker[20], it was freezing. Camped about 120 miles south of Belgrade.

---

20 *The Canadian told them he was on his way to his wedding the following day and was really worried he would not make it on time. My dad, Marius, a cart with water buffalo helped to pull him out.*

Stop for tea in Yugoslavia

Monday, 7th April 1958

As described by Audrey in her diary:

"Our camp was dry but really cold, 35°F when we woke. We are watched doing our usual chores by about 10 farm children supposedly on their way to school. They wore thick homespun woolen breeches, cloth caps and rubber shoes. An older boy came and offered us a light red wine and Marius gave him two cigarettes. We drove off and about an hour and half later found the abandoned Studebaker at the side of the road with a back blowout. We looked for our Canadian but didn't see him. As we drove towards Nis the road improved. All the towns have cobblestones and we met endless carts and horses or cows or bullocks or water buffalos carrying market goods. The women were all wearing embroidered national costumes in the town. Headscarves, sometimes leather jurkens and rubber shoes, many lacy petticoats and the embroidered on black aprons to finish it. The animals were beautiful. We had no time to stop and take photos, great pity. Beyond Nis the road was tarred and good. Overcast weather

on a wintery scene. Camped about 30 miles south of Beograd (Belgrade) in a dip by the road. Wind was terribly cold. At dusk saw our Canadian bridegroom go past in his Studebaker, already one day late for his wedding. Got out winter boots and woolies."

Yugoslavian countryside

Tuesday, 8th April 1958

Up at 5:20 am as I was so cold in bed. Made coffee and tried to warm up moving around. Had breakfast. The car would not start as it was too cold. Audrey and I went for a walk to warm up while the boys battled. They had still not got it started by the time we got back. Carel eventually found out that there was no petrol!!! Laugh. When we finally got the Kombi going she got stuck in the mud. We tried pushing her out but it was uphill and we didn't make much progress. While we were struggling a cart and two horses arrived on the scene and the driver very kindly turned back to help us. The horses pulled the Kombi up the hill with ease, we sighed a sigh of relief. The delay cost us two hours of precious travelling time. Travelled on through many small picturesque villages reaching Belgrade at 11:30 am. It was bitterly cold and raining. We put on our macs and walked around the city trying to get supplies. What a job as nearly all the shopkeepers couldn't understand English or German. After a lot of battling we managed, food is very expensive. We only bought bread, margarine, cheese and vegetables and four eggs. We can't afford meat so from now on we are going to eat bread and spaghetti and vegetables. It's going to be a bit of a battle trying to keep the boys satisfied but they will just have to pull in their belts. Didn't see much of Belgrade, it was too cold and we were in a hurry. Saw a wonderful bridge across the river with very big spans. Also an ancient castle surrounded by a very big wall. A few miles out of Belgrade on the autobahn we stopped for lunch. It was terribly cold and I nearly froze. Had on all my warm clothes and fur boots but it didn't seem to help. On the autobahn we bypassed all villages but we could see them in the distance, their little churches always stood out very clearly. Passed through big forests of birch trees flooded with water from the melting snow. It made a lovely picture. Camped alongside the autobahn, it was very cold. Audrey cooked, Carel and I sat and talked.

Kombi pulled up the hill

Horses help pull combi up the hill

Bridge in Yugoslavia

Yugoslavia roads

Wednesday, 9th April 1958 (Thel's Birthday)

Up very early as we have a long way to go to reach the border, it is the last day of our transit visa. It was bitterly cold, the windows of the Kombi were all frozen over and the water had a layer of ice on top. We each had a fried egg for breakfast, it was so nice. Got on the road at 7:20 am, I had a run before getting in the car so I was a bit warmer than the rest. The sun tried to shine and at times came through the clouds but not for long. The little farms alongside the road were lovely, each with its barn (tiled with red tiles), haystacks, geese, and fowls. The horses and cows all look wonderfully fat. They use both their horses and cows for ploughing or pulling carts. There was still a lot of water from the melted snow lying around, the land is not well drained. We by-passed Zagreb, a big industrial town and turned off the autobahn to travel down to Rijeka. This stretch was really beautiful – mountainous. It was a sunny day so everything was looking like spring. The little villages are very picturesque. Saw plenty of snow high up in the mountains amongst the fir trees, plenty of primroses in the valleys. Stopped for lunch next to a river, very beautiful, passed by a lake where we stopped to take photos and play in the snow. Carel chased me and I fell on the road – result holes in my slacks and knees. We nearly ran out of petrol so we freewheeled all the way down to Rijeka. We parked the car and walked around the town. Posted some letters then Carel and I walked around the harbour, saw women loading a ship!! Took some lovely photos of the small fishing boats moored on a canal. Bought vegetables and bread, bread very fresh, we ate it walking along the street. Audrey, Carel and I were rash enough to buy ourselves each a cake – we sat and ate it in the shop and enjoyed it. Travelled about 10 miles, went through Customs and into Italy. Camped in a pine forest very near the border, it is bitterly cold.

Ryjika and the boats

Ryjika, Yugoslavia

Near Trieste, forest campsite

Thursday, 10th April 1958

Woke at 6 am and it was snowing. Audrey and I lay in bed for a while and watched it. It was coming down so gently, the first snow I have ever seen. Made breakfast and then Carel and I went for a walk in the forest to see the snow. Not much had fallen only enough to show white but it was so nice walking along while the flakes were coming down. Everything was so quiet. Packed up and drove into Trieste. A very big beautiful peaceful city. The streets are very wide and the traffic well ordered. We parked the car at the station and then walked around. Cashed some money then Audrey and I separated from the boys and did some shopping. The shops were well stocked but we didn't have much money so we just looked. Bought some food and then met the boys again. Carvings and statues are very beautiful. Walked across quite a few squares where there were street cafés and hundreds of pigeons. Carel, Audrey and I walked around looking for tourist badges. Bought a bottle of Italian wine in a fancy bottle. Drove along the coast past the harbour and had onion sandwich lunch parked overlooking the sea and a fashionable bathing pavilion. The sun was shining but the wind was very cold. We all had our big coats on. Drove around and had a look at the city, very narrow cobbled streets. Lost our way looking for Richard's Arch, passed the old Roman Theatre. Walked around the piazza dell'unita with some wonderful buildings of fine mosaics and statues. Drove out of Trieste and had a look at the Miramare Castle. The gardens were well laid out and we spent a good 1 ½ hours walking around. Watched the swans in the pond, two big black ones as well as six white ones, beautiful birds. Plenty of statues in the gardens. Couldn't get into the castle as we were too late. Drove on towards Venice. Camped and Carel serviced the car, reverse gear had gone when we tried getting out of a pebbled part of the road. It was raining and was bitterly cold. Had supper and went to bed shivering.

Friday, 11th April 1958

Woke early and got up. Gosh but Audrey takes an age to do anything. She started long before I did but only finished after I had made coffee. It was very cold, 40°F only 8°F above freezing. Put on all my warm clothes. Travelled on towards Venice. Passed through many villages, each one having its own big church beautifully set and ornaments with big statues of Christ and the Madonna. We also saw a lot of shrines. We arrived in Venice in the rain at 10:20 am. It was bitterly cold, wind and sleet. Parked the car and Audrey, Carel and I walked around looking for some bread. Went back to the car and sat and ate our lunch in the car. Then we all put on Macs, boots and caps and set off to the ferry stop to catch the ferry to the Piazza of St Marks. We had to wait and nearly froze, never thought I would see Venice in such weather. We managed to get seats on the ferry but could see very little as it was raining very hard. Travelled up the Grand Canal and saw gondolas moored in strings, they looked very sad in the wet weather. The ferry travelled very fast and smoothly. We walked from the ferry stop to the Piazza San Marco, what a wonderful place and that even in the rain. We had to stick to the pavements to keep out of the rain. Very beautiful pieces of Vincentian glass to be had for next to nothing. Audrey and I really enjoyed the window shopping. After walking around the Piazza we went into the church of St Mark. I can't describe it, it was too wonderful. I have never seen such a wonderful place, the gold mosaics and paintings were too beautiful. Only sorry the ceilings weren't lit up more. The golden altar back was something out of this world. I want to go back and see it again. Went into a glass factory and watched them blowing glass animals and beads, it is so very interesting. Walked to the French Consulate to get our visas. All in and out of the canals, very enlightening but cold as it was raining. Walked back to the car, found a wonderful camp spot, it snowed.

Saturday, 12th April 1958

Woke up to the sound of peeling bells, lay and listened to them for a long time. Had a good breakfast. It was bitterly cold below freezing point. Drove to the Piazza Roma and parked the car. Took a ferry to the Piazza San Marco. Walked around the Piazza, booked for the glass blowing. Fed the pigeons, there were hundreds of them. Audrey and I enjoyed it and Carel took some photos of us feeding the birds. It was still raining so we went into the Ducale's Palace. Spent four hours going around it. The paintings were marvellous and the ceiling and sculptures magnificent, I thoroughly enjoyed it. How they painted such big canvasses beats me. Went into the dungeons and then walked across the bridge of Sighs. Walked along the Grand Canal, bought some bread which we ate for lunch. Marius left us to go and have something to drink, we couldn't afford anything. Went into the glass factory, very interesting they are born artists. Walked around the showroom saw some of the most beautiful pieces I have ever seen, the colours and shapes were wonderful. Walked back to the car, very sad because we couldn't afford anything from the factory. Very interesting walk along the canals and over the bridges. Back to our camp.

Joan and Audrey in St Mark's Square, Venice

Sunday, 13th April 1958

Got up early and it is very cold and still raining. We packed up and left Lugano campground just after 8 am. Hope the next time I visit Venice the sun will be shinning. Travelled on the autostrada from Venice to Padua. Couldn't see much due to rain. From Padua we continued through Verona, bypassed Brescia and Milan. A real pity as we had intended to spend the day at Milan. Had lunch sitting in the Kombi parked on the shore of a small lake. All the mountains on the other side of the lake were covered in snow. Very cold and misty. Travelled from Milan to Torinto (Turin) on the autostrada, very misty saw just about nothing. My knee was aching. Camped in a snowfield alongside the road just outside of Torinto (Turin) on the way to Susa – very cold. Supper and to bed, all in the Kombi.

Carel and Audrey

Monday, 14th April 1958

Had a very good night – Audrey, Carel and I slept in the back and Marius on the front seat. We all were warm, but the tent had collapsed during the night. Still raining when we woke and Audrey got up and made coffee and breakfast. Packed up in the rain, we're getting a bit tired of the wet. It was so cold with all the fields covered in snow. Arrived at Susa in a snowstorm. Bought provisions to spend all our Italian money. Walked around looking for the post office. Found that the main road to Lyon was closed due to heavy snowfall last night so we had to travel around via Briancon. The scenery was terrific, all the country was covered in snow. Had lunch overlooking a snow filled valley just out of Oulx. It was perfect. The sun shone and we enjoyed its warmth. Had bread rolls and cheese, terrific with hot coffee. Crossed the border into France at Claviere. It was bitterly cold there, windy and snowing. Carel did all the paperwork and we sat in the car. Between Briancon and camping we struck very heavy snow drifts on the mountain passes. Sometimes they were over 10 ft high alongside the road. We even had a blizzard and got stuck along with quite a few other cars. A snow plough was blocking the road and by standing still a while the tyres iced up and when we wanted to continue they just slipped on the ice. Anyway the boys got out and pushed us off, poor things they were covered in snow when they got into the car again. Passed many skiing villages with very picturesque hotels. Mostly built on the Swiss chalet lines, lovely wooden work. Also saw plenty of ski lifts and skiers, it all looked so nice, made me feel like trying skiing myself. We camped next to an old house alongside a street, all amongst the snow. Had supper, Audrey cooked and I wrote letters. Very cold. Carel made a fire and we sat round it warning ourselves and drying out our shoes[21].

France border crossing

[21] *Marius decided to wash ALL his clothing in a nearby stream. On his return he tripped and ended up in the water drenching the clothing he was wearing which was also his only set of dry clothes much to the amusement of the others.*

Alps scenery

French Alps and campsite by old farm house

Tuesday, 15th April 1958

Up early and made coffee. The sun was shining and I stood outside in the sun drinking my coffee. What a beautiful sight, the sun on the snow on the mountains, it was so nice to feel the warmth of the sun again. After breakfast Audrey and I decided to wash our hair. Mine was very dirty, last washed 3½ weeks ago. The boys also had a hair wash and we managed to dry out all our wet things. We got on the road again at 10 am. Travelled through the mountains, beautiful scenery, the snow on the mountains and the rivers in the valleys. We motored through quite a few tunnels. All the houses in the mountains are painted very bright colours and look very nice. When we reached the plains, we saw plenty of signs of spring. All the trees were in blossom with plenty of young green leaves. The countryside looked so new. Bought some fresh bread in a small village and ate lunch in the car just outside of Grenoble. It was raining again. We enjoyed the bread and cheese. Beyond Grenoble it stopped raining. All the famers were busy working in the lands. What lovely big farm horses they have. Passed by some lovely old Chateaux. It started raining again just before we reached Lyon. Carel and I had a bit of an argument over posting a letter. He wanted to bypass Lyon and I wanted to go in to post my letter. After a bit of a clash of wills he posted my letter. I know it was stupid, wish the other two were not with us then could have had it out, would have been better for both of us. Left Lyon in the rain, a very big city with well-organised traffic. Passed through a tunnel 1½ miles long just outside of Lyon, it was well lit and beautifully tiled. Travelled through very fertile farming country. Tried to camp in a campground but couldn't find anyone to help us. Camped alongside the road, very cold and raining. We nearly froze. Carel, Audrey and I slept inside Marius outside with our extra blanket.

Wednesday, 16th April 1958

Up early as we want to get to Paris tonight or at least near Paris. Still raining and very cold. A real pity that we couldn't see very much as we were travelling through beautiful farm country. Bought bread and vegetables along the way. Travelled on through Macon, Chalon, Avalon, Auxerre – a beautiful old church in the city centre. Sat and ate lunch in the car parked in the middle of a big forest. The sun came out while we were in Auxerre, quite warm. What a difference, the country immediately became interesting. All the farmers are very busy in their lands. The villages are all a hive of activity and have very neatly laid out gardens with plenty of spring flowers, plenty of blossoms too. Drove off the main road into Fontainebleau. The Palace is very beautiful, saw the swans on the moat water. Stopped and bought some postcards as we couldn't stay longer. Camped about 20 miles out of Paris in an old quarry. Carel greased the car, Audrey cooked and I wrote letters. Very cold wind.

Thursday, 17th April 1958

Up early washed and dressed ready for Paris. I was quite excited. We seemed to drive for miles before coming to the Seine. Gosh but the traffic moves fast, everyone drives at 40 mph. How all the cars sort themselves out amazed me. We crossed the Seine and travelled up the Champs Elysees passing the statue of Juliet, Bastille Obelisk of Luxor, the Louvre and up to the Arc de Triomphe. Parked near the Arc and went to the South African Embassy. It was very hot inside. They helped us by telling us where we could camp. Bought some food, all very expensive except for the margarine. Drove out to our camp which is a lovely spot right on the river bank. Cost us 1650 Franc for three nights. Paris was looking terrific. It was a dull day and a bit nippy but all the trees were just getting their leaves, such soft green. We ate lunch and then pitched camp. There were plenty of other campers on the ground. We put on our coats and started out to catch the Metro to central Paris. Just out of the campground gates we were given a lift by an American gentleman in a Mercedes Benz. Gosh could he talk and was he ignorant. Audrey and my hair stood on end at the sweeping statements he made. Walked around central Paris. How I loved it, there was so much to see. The women were very smart and had hair all colours. Audrey and I walked around staring. On the whole everything in the shops was most expensive, one wonders how the French manage to live. Went to American Express to draw money, what smart offices. Audrey and I went over the Church of St Mary Magdalene. Very beautiful statues all around the outside of the church, Inside it was so very quiet that we didn't dare to walk around too much. Sat on the steps outside waiting for Carel. Watched the traffic going up and down the Champs Elysees. It was too fantastic. Went back to camp in the Metro (the underground), it's a wonderful service. Had to walk from the Port de Neulling to the camp two miles away. Met some Americans in camp and also looked over a Kombi camper that was very smart. Talked and then bed, it is still very cold.

Friday, 18th April 1958

Mum's birthday, happy birthday Mum. Got up early to do some washing. My legs were still tired from yesterday's walking. Walked and caught the Metro. Went to the Belgian Consulate for visas, a lot of people there and we had to wait. Audrey and I decided to leave the boys and walk down the Champs Elysees. Carel was to wait for the visas. What an interesting walk. Looked in the window of all the smart dress shops, what beauties and what prices £36 for a simple frock.

Beautiful shoes at £6–10 a pair. Went into a departmental store and looked around, things were just as expensive. Bought some chocolate. Walked across the Place de la Concorde, such beautiful statues representing the eight larger French cities. Continued through the gardens Jordin des Tuileries. The trees where beautiful with their new buds. The birds' fish in the ponds and the ducks are all part of it. The statues in the gardens were fantastic, never seen anything like it before. Met Carel at the small Arc de Triomphe and from there we walked around the Louvre and along the banks of the Seine. Tried to buy some bread but couldn't find a bakery. We walked to the Church of Notre Dome. Found a bakery nearby – bought bread and then ate lunch (bread, cheese and chocolate) sitting on the steps of the bridge leading down to the Seine at Notre Dame. The sun shone and we enjoyed our site, the walking does tire one. Went into Notre Dame. What a beautiful church, the stain glass windows were perfect. Only drawback was not enough light in the church to appreciate the paintings. All the side chapels have beautiful statues. Beautiful columns inside the main body of the church. Climbed the tower, a wonderful view of Paris from the top. The sun was shining and we could see for miles around. The church is built in the shape of a cross and has beautiful carving. Dressed for supper, dress a bit crumple and had all our petticoats for warmth, then went to the Moulin Rouge Night Club. The show was good, good acts in between the nude chorus girls who weren't so hot. Cost us £6, but we had to leave early to catch the Metro, only just made it back to camp. Glad we went.

Carel in Paris

Eiffel Tower

Saturday, 19th April 1958

What a job getting out of bed, late nights are so few these days. After breakfast Carel, Audrey and I went into Paris. Carel left us and Audrey and I went to the Louvre. We spent 3½ hours inside and only managed to cover one wing. Saw the Venus de Milo, the Mona Lisa. The paintings were really excellent. Sorry we did not have time to see more. Met Carel at the Arc de Triomphe. We were all very tired and foot sore. Ate lunch, bread and cheese, sitting in the park in front of the Louvre. The sun was shining and I enjoyed feeding the pigeons. Carel spoilt us and gave us each an apple, the first since Greece, most enjoyable. Tired or not we decided to walk to the Eiffel Tower.

Quiet a walk especially as we were all so tired. The park at the Tower was very beautiful, all the trees with new leaves, blossoms and spring flowers. Also all the children at play and the mothers sitting knitting. The Eiffel Tower sure is big, an amazing feat of engineering. Carel and I walked around on our own, Audrey was too tired. Caught the Metro back to camp. Had to buy food at Nevilly which we had to carry for 1¾ miles – what a tough walk I was nearly dead by the time we reached camp. Met some other South Africans in camp, the Slabberts from Cape Town, a very nice young couple. After supper we took the tent off the Kombi and all piled in and went to see the lights of Paris, it was wonderful. The statues and buildings looked much better lit up. Had coffee with the Slabberts and then went to bed – another late night.

Sunday, 20th April 1958

Got up early and packed to leave Paris. Went to say cheerio to the Slabberts. Carel and I washed the car quickly while everyone was talking. Boy took some cine shots of us. Left camp at 9:30 am. Travelled about 20 miles out of Paris when the car started giving trouble. Stopped and while Carel worked on the car wrote letters. It was a glorious sunny day. Ate lunch and then moved on. The countryside looked wonderful, everything was so green. Passed many beautiful churches. Traveled through Senlis. Compiegne, Soissons, Loan Vervins, Maubeuge, Mons and arriving in Brussels at 8:10 pm. The Kombi is still playing up and backfiring. A chap on a scooter showed us the camp ground, it was the ground around some schools playing fields. We were all tired, had supper and went to bed, not so cold.

Monday, 21st April 1958

What a job getting out of bed, I was so tired. Carel worked on the car as the gearbox is giving trouble. Packed up and drove to the 1958 World Fair. Marius was driving and got us all involved in a car park miles from the Fair so we had to catch a bus to the Fair. We three were a bit fed up as it meant wasting money on bus fares. Arrived at the main gates of the Fair just after 10 am. What tremendous structures they have built, they are expecting thousands of people and cars. The main entrance hall was tremendous with a canvas roof. There were banks, post offices, shops, information, daylight hotels, cafés, hairdressers etc there. We changed money, got a map of the Fair and then set off. As one comes out of the glass doors into the Fair one gets a wonderful view of the Atrium and fountains. We decided to walk around and pick out which Pavilions we wanted to see and then come back tomorrow. We were also looking for bread and couldn't find any. Some of the Pavilions were very futuristic in design, steel tubing and glass being the main materials used. The German Pavilion really impressed us with its big hanging bridge. The lakes and fountains were beautiful and every bank was covered with grass and flowers. The daffodils were particularly beautiful. We left the Fair at 3 pm very tired and hungry. Bought some bread and went to look for a camp spot. Found one near the canals. Ate lunch there and then went into Brussels to book our passages on the Canal ferry and have a look at Brussels. Parked the car in a beautiful square surrounded by old buildings decorated with gold figurines. Walked around passing some lovely old churches. Went to see the statue Manneke Pis, he is a chubby little fellow. Hung around waiting for the lights to come on. It was cold but worth it as they had special decorations up. I enjoyed it all, camped very late and to bed after supper.

Brussels

Tuesday, 22nd April 1958

These late nights are not good, it's a battle getting up in the morning. My leg is giving me trouble, it needs a rest. After breakfast I made up a picnic lunch, we're not being caught again. Got to the Fair just after 10 am. Marius went his own way while Carel, Audrey and I set off together. Went through the Gardens of the Four Seasons which was beautifully laid out with levelling dancing fountains. Watched them making chocolate at quite a few of the Pavilions and then bought some choc at Cote d'Or. Went over Dixon steel supports, very interesting. Climbed a few of the fantastic shaped structures and watched miniature cars travelling across a map of Belgium. Went into the Folklore section, cost us 5/- and we were most disappointed. It consisted mostly of national houses and cafés and there wasn't much happening when we were there. It would have been lovely at night. At 1 pm we met for lunch, potatoes in jackets sausages but forgot the jam!, which we ate sitting on a bench overlooking the Fair. The music was terrific, the Belgium National Band, so nice to hear good music played well. After lunch we all split up and went our own way. I sat and wrote letters for just over an hour. My leg was sore and I needed the rest. Walked around the gardens, they were lovely. Went through the Spanish section, also quite good. The British Pavilion was excellent and I spent over an hour there, everything was so well explained. Watched an artificial heart working, very interesting. Saw TV for the first time. Went into the United States Pavilion, a tremendous circular structure. Everything was set out well, watched a Mannequin parade. Went into the Russian Pavilion but couldn't understand a thing, everything was written in Russian. The art section was excellent, also the ballet. Met up with the others for supper. Had a rest until the lights came on. What a wonderful sight at night. The main fountain was perfect, all coloured, and the Atrium was lit up like stars. Walked around for about two hours, it was just too perfect. I've never seen such a fairyland of lights, the fountains were out of this world. Camped very tired but happy.

Carel and Audrey at the Expo, Brussels

Wednesday, 23rd April 1958

Drove into Brussels to have another look at the city. Drove to the Palace of Justice where we had a wonderful view of the city. Left Brussels just after 12 pm. Had lunch sitting on a grass bank. The sun was so nice and warm. All along the way the garages and cafés and hotels were decorated with flags and bunting, everything was so gay. We were travelling through heavily built-up area. Passed through Anvers, Breda, Utrecht and our first windmill. We stopped at Utrecht, did a quick change into skirts, and Carel took us to a Chinese restaurant for supper. It was called the "Fuhien". We had a very nice meal of a bean preparation, fried rice, eggs and sticks of meat like our South African braaivleis dish sousarties. I ate more than I should but it was so nice. We left Utrecht, after 1½ hours to 2 hours stop, and travelled onto Amsterdam. All the Dutch houses are so neat and clean. We parked the car and walked around Amsterdam. There were a lot of people in the streets. I wanted to spend 1d but we couldn't find a lav. Finally Audrey and I went into a cinema, after we got inside, we discovered we had no money – laugh – Audrey left me and went to fetch some money from Carel. There was so much to see in the streets. Plenty of people. The souvenir shops were very interesting, things were cheap, so sorry that I haven't any spare money to buy presents. We walked all in and around the canals and crossed over some very pretty bridges. Carel wanted to show us the dancing fountains but we couldn't find it. We were all tired so we walked back to the car. Drove out of town to camp. Found a very nice spot alongside the canal. Made some tea and then went to bed. The days spent in the cities are really very tiring.

Thursday, 24th April 1958

Up early and gave everyone breakfast in bed. Drove into Amsterdam and parked the car. We split up. Audrey went shopping, Marius went off and Carel and I set off for the Rijksmuseum. The streets of Amsterdam are very pretty and neat. Plenty of flowers and the trees are just beginning to get green. We spent 1½ hours in the Museum and only went through the section of old Dutch Masters. I thoroughly enjoyed myself and so did Carel. Saw a lot of Steen, Hals, Rembrandt and Vermeer work, which I love. Rembrandt's Nachtwacht is terrific and very well placed, could have sat for hours looking at it. We walked from the Rijksmuseum to central Amsterdam and on the way we passed a street Organ, a big push musical box very gaily painted. It is played very like a Panola only the man turns a handle instead of pedalling it. The music was so nice and Carel and

I stood for quite a while on a canal bridge listening to it. We did a bit of shopping for bits and pieces, the shops were so interesting. The silverware was too terrific, would have loved to buy some. We went into a self-service café for tea. I had hot chocolate and a fruitcake and Carel had coffee and chips and it cost us 2/6d which was very reasonable considering prices in Europe. Walked back to the car where we had lunch and parked in the middle of Frederick Square. People don't seem to worry about that sort of thing here. After lunch we went on a canal motor boat, cost us 2/6d each for 1½ hours. It was a very interesting trip, the sun was shining and we could see all around as the whole of the top of the boat was glass. Our guide was interesting and full of jokes too. The pilot of the boat knew his job well, some of the canals are very narrow and have sharp corners. After we landed again, we did some shopping and then set off for Keukenhof. It was cold, saw quite a lot of tulips. Camped just outside Keukenhof, did some washing.

Amsterdam boat cruise

Friday, 25th April 1958

Woke up to the sound of rain. All the washing was dripping wet. I was so disappointed as I wanted to see all the flowers. Went to sleep again but woke as

Audrey was getting dressed. She gave us breakfast in bed. It was cold and the rain was pelting down, it was so cosy inside the Kombi. We lay for a while and then packed up and drove to Keukenhof. Audrey and I packed a picnic lunch, by the time we had finished the rain had stopped and that after we had taken out our macs etc. What a wonderful time we had in Keukenhof. The flowers were too beautiful. I've never seen such big daffodils or such variety. The hyacinths were just out of this world all colours, big and giving off a terrific scent. We walked all over the place and sat and ate our lunch near the windmill. By this time the sun was shining, it was very pleasant. Climbed the windmill. Took plenty of photos, hope they come out well. The birds were singing, it was most pleasant. The cars in the car park bore registration plates from just about every country in Europe. Plenty of US Forces in German cars, they seem to be travelling all over Europe. We left Keukenhof and travelled down to Den Haag. Passed many fields of tulips and daffodils – just a maze of colour. It was so nice. Arrived in the Den Haag just after 4 pm. Carel drove us around the city and showed us some of the sights. The promenade at Scheveningen seaside resort, the Royal Palace, the Vredespaleis and many other landmarks. We found a nice camp spot where they were building some new houses. Carel worked on the car again. Hung out all the wet washing, there was a lovely strong wind blowing. Sat and talked for a while after supper. By the time we were in bed the wind was blowing real cold but it was so warm inside. Started raining later.

Saturday, 26th April 1958

What a good thing I took the washing in, it was raining cats and dogs and so cold. Packed up and set off for Ostend. We passed by Madurodam the miniature town but as it was raining we didn't go in. At Delft we stopped to buy an ice cream which was very nice. Ate lunch in the car outside Rotterdam. What a pity it was raining so hard, didn't see very much, also very cold. Turned off the main road at Antwerp towards Gent and Ostend. Drove around Ostend looking for a camp spot – saw their "gross-clock" which was very interesting. Camped in a campground. Very cold the wind blew hard all night.

Sunday, 27th April 1958

The tent nearly blew down during the night. Woke early and dressed, it was so cold. Arrived at the docks just at 8 am. Got on board with very little trouble. The crossing was rough and I stayed sitting in one place all the time. Watched the Whites Cliffs of Dover approach. Got off the boat without any trouble. Ate lunch in the Customs sheds much to everyone's amusement. Left Dover for London, so nice to see English adverts and signs again. Everything green and in blossom saw many lambs. Travelled through Canterbury, saw many hop fields. Camped about 40 miles south of London.

Loading the Kombi, Ostend

Monday, 28th April 1958

Slept very well especially after last night's disturbed evening. Woke late with the result that we couldn't have a proper wash. Travelled the last 40 miles to London. It was really exciting reading all the English signs and adverts, quite like home. Took some photos as we reached the first London signboard. We drove for miles through London suburbs before we came to London Bridge. I couldn't believe I was really driving over it. Tower Bridge was on our right and the sun was just shinning. Arrived at Trafalgar Square via Stand Street. We parked the car very near Admiralty Arch and took some more photos. Took some with the South Africa house in the background just to finish off the tour. Audrey and I stayed with the car and the boys went to register at South Africa House. Then we drove up the Mall past Buckingham Palace, Constitution Hill,

Brompton Road and then straight on to Earls Court. We parked the car and walked around looking for the club. We soon found it. We were very heartily welcomed which was so nice. We also had quite a big mail waiting for us, a lovely long read. The Club had booked us in at Craig House which was just over the road from the Club. Carel fetched the Kombi and we parked right in front of the club. We had a bit of a battle unpacking, didn't really know where to start. After much sorting out we moved our clothes into our room. Audrey and I together on the 1st floor and the boys together on the 3rd floor. Had a terrific hot bath. Scrubbed myself from head to foot, it was so nice. We ate lunch sitting in the car. Wrote letters in the afternoon and generally got ourselves organised. Went over to the club and sat in the lounge for a while, met quite a few club members, all very interested in our trip. Had supper at the club, it was very nice and only cost us 4/6d each for soup, chop, peas, potatoes and ice cream. Watched them dancing in the Globe Trotters Room for a while but not much room to move. Went to bed early. Very happy after four months of terrific travelling.

End of the road: Joan, Marius, Carel and Audrey, London

London arrival

OVC, Earls court, London

Tuesday, 29th April 1958

Woke early and went and had another hot bath – not because I felt dirty, but just to enjoy the hot water. Finished off my letter to mum and then went over to the club for breakfast. Had our first big breakfast since leaving home. Egg and bacon, toast, marmalade and tea – we all enjoyed it. After breakfast we sorted out our washing and took it to the club laundry – cost 1/6d for 9 lbs. Then we set about looking for some cheaper boarding. Craig House was costing us 12/6d for bed and breakfast. We got some addresses from the club and then set out. The first one wasn't so good but we took the second lot. Two double rooms at 24 Longridge Road at £4-4-0 a week. They are both big rooms each with a gas ring for cooking. We have free use of the bathroom. So we checked out of Craig House packed up and moved. What a business. Anyway we soon got ourselves sorted out. Fetched all our cooking utensils from the car and set up home, I'm sure we will be very happy here. Audrey and I each have a big and a small drawer and half the wardrobe. Did some shopping at the supermarket. Things are certainly much cheaper here in England as compared with Europe. But they are still on the high side as compared with South Africa. Only hope we can stick to the pace and still live well. Money is going to be very tight. Cooked my first meal on a gas cooker. Went very well indeed and is very quick. We sat down at the table to eat; it was so strange looking across the table at Carel after four months of camp life. Sat chatting for a while then the boys washed the dishes. Finished writing letters – Carel finished off our accounts and we discussed them.

Cape Town to Khartoum:	£48-19-6 (5)
Khartoum to Alex:	£36-19-3 (3)
Alex to Greece:	£ 9-13-2 (3)
Greece to London:	£24-15-4 (4)
Each	£120-7-3

Not bad considering we were on the road for four months and travelled just over 13,500 miles.

My Mom's diary continued to describe her daily activities in London, weekend fun, work and other day to day stuff. Within a week or two the daily recordings became briefer, then days were skipped and only interesting weekend activity recorded. Of note though is the below two entries, as written in the diary.

Thursday, 19th June 1958

Announced our engagement.

Saturday, 26th July 1958

Our wedding day.

Carel and Joan's wedding day, London

The newly-weds, London

After the Trip

Carel and Joan (ex Povall) Marais

Joan got a job as a clerk/bookkeeper in a fashion shoe store in Knightsbridge in early May. Carel left London in August working for a UK firm in Blantyre Malawi building a water supply for the capital. Joan later joined Carel in Blantyre. They continued on to Lagos Nigeria where Carel was building national roads and was the soil mechanic's specialist. Thereafter they ended up in South West Africa (Namibia) with more soil evaluations, road building and identifying the new site for the commercial and military airport for Windhoek. They returned to South Africa in the mid 1960s, shortly after they started a family raising two sons and a daughter. They retired to Knysna, South Africa.

Audrey (ex Nives) van Eeden

Audrey remained in London and started working as a draughts woman for an Architectural firm in Green Park mid-May. She also studied 1st year Architecture during this time. She returned to South Africa end 1959, engaged to a South African met in London, married, became a South African citizen (she was British born and educated) and they started a family raising two sons and a daughter. Audrey continued her art and had a number of successful exhibits. They retired to Jeffreys Bay, South Africa.

Marius Marais

Marius began work for the Manchester London Roadway leaving London for Rugby Warwickshire in June. He remained in England working on the roadways. This lasted about a year and then he accepted a job back in Phalaborwa South Africa on the mines where he remained until he retired to Cape Town, South Africa. Marius was a bachelor his whole life and never had children.

Johan Marais

Johan married the girl he flew back for, started his career and settled in Johannesburg South Africa. They started a family raising two sons. Sadly Johan passed away from lung cancer while his youngest son was in his final year of school at the age of 58.

Carel, Audrey, Joan and Marius in December 1999, during a reunion in Knysna

CPSIA information can be obtained
at www.ICGtesting.com
Printed in the USA
BVHW051231260421
605864BV00014B/1782

9 781528 997652